एक आदर्श शिक्षक की जीवन यात्रा

LIFE JOURNEY OF AN IDEAL TEACHER

शिक्षा एवं सामाजिक कार्यों में योगदान के 60 वर्ष

60 YEARS OF CONTRIBUTION TO EDUCATION AND SOCIAL WORKS

स्वर्गीय श्री केशव प्रसाद अम्बष्ठ

LATE SHRI KESHAV PRASAD AMBSTA

लेखक:
डॉ. गौरव कुमार
(बेल्जियम)

AUTHOR:
DR. GAURAV KUMAR
(BELGIUM)

INDIA • SINGAPORE • MALAYSIA

ISBN 979-8-89277-307-2

Disclaimers

Intents of this book is collection of memoirs of author's father as his legacy.

View and contents presented in this book is true based on author's limited knowledge and collection from his own memory, observations, and information obtained from members of his family, relatives and people from village, ex-colleagues and teachers known to his father. People may or may not agree partially or fully with views and information in this book.

Personal experience expressed by several people and their photo in this book have given their consent to publish it and have been collected in their handwritten notes via WhatsApp.

Sh. Keshav Prasad Ambsta and Smt Rukmini Kumari

Contents

Part 1 English Version

(पृष्ठ संख्या 60 से हिंदी संस्करण)

Part 2 हिंदी

Part 1 English Version

(पृष्ठ संख्या 60 से हिंदी संस्करण)

Fig 2. Sketch of the favorite flower (merigold) drawn by Yash - tribute by Yash Pratyush Ambsta (Grandson) to his Dada Ji

Background/Foreword

A biography for a father, teacher, mentor, social and humanitarian worker, who dedicated his entire life for the social, moral, educational and female empowerment services to bring positive changes in the 21st century in rural India. Recently, a heart touching headline caught my attention in a prominent newspaper: "Unsung heroes: 20 Padma Shri awardees who have remained unknown, until now." This resonated deeply with me, as I firmly believe in the existence of numerous individuals in our community who, without seeking glory and fame, contribute selflessly for the well-being of society. Among these unsung heroes, I am confident that my father (Papa) stands as a prime example, unselfishly dedicating himself in making a positive impact on the lives of those around him.

Born in a poor family in a remote village of Bihar, he struggled and fought for education, empowered himself and his family and transformed the lives of hundreds of people via education and teaching. During his tenure of 37 years as a headmaster, he was an amazing teacher who did more than just his job. He was honest and cared a lot about teaching his students. He did more than teaching the curriculum, he also encouraged and helped them and their families to believe in the power of education. He believed in making sure girls received a good education, especially when the rural society thought it wasn't essential during mid to late 1970s. This was during a time when the literacy rates were lower and many girls weren't encouraged to go to school in Bihar because of social barriers against gender equality.

What amazed me the most was how energetic he was even at the age of 80 years. After retiring from his work in 2002 at the age of 60, I've always seen him so active and conscious about his health, diet and exercise. He walked frequently, even rode his bicycle for short distances. Whenever we talked, he told me he was busy in education work at the Girls School in our village. More often than not he was their helping school staff with admissions, coaching, teaching, or any other school-related administrative tasks. He wasn't just dedicated to the students; he also helped the teachers with their everyday jobs. He kept doing all of this until his very last day on March 4, 2023. The teachers always said this "he had a mindset to bring a solution for every problem".

Witnessing his vitality and commitment at such an advanced age left a profound impression on me. His tireless efforts inspired the lives and families of many, fostering growth and success. As his son, I feel a profound duty to immortalize his legacy through this biography, with the hope that it will serve as a tribute and inspiration for generations to come.

Overview of his life Journey

1943: Born on 1st Jan, 1943

1959: Completed middle school board exam (Madhepura)

1962: Married with Amma Smt. Rukmini Kumari.

1963: Completed Bachelore of Arts(BA) (GD College, Begusarai, Bhagalpur University)

1963: Joined as a temporary teacher in school, Paharichak, Sonpur.

1965: Joined as a headmaster in middle school, Paharichak, Sonpur.

1975: Diploma in Teaching (Bihar Vishwavidhalay)

1980: Master of Arts (MA) in Political Sciences)Bihar Vishwavidhalay)

2002: Retired after 40 years of service

His last day: 04 March, 2023

Let me share the story of Papa's life, starting from March 4, 2023, which was a significant day. It's important because he passed away peacefully. It was as if he achieved a state of deep meditation or Samadhi without experiencing any pain or suffering on his last day. He was not bed ridden or sick and didn't have any serious disease except high BP. He was active and healthy at the age of 80.

It was a Saturday morning. He followed his daily routine, waking up at 6 am. After doing all his daily activities and Yoga, he took bath and got ready to read our holiest book "Ramayan", something he had been doing every Saturday for the past 30 years.

After his prayer session 9-10 am, where he read the Ramayan for about 30-40 minutes, he played a holy conch (Shankha). Once he finished his prayers, he left the praying area with incense in his hand and gave it to Amma (my mother). As she went into the room to place the incense, she heard a sound. Hurrying back, she found Papa lying on the floor, unconscious. Despite trying to revive him and seeking help from a neighbor, his soul peacefully left his body without any pain or suffering within 2-3 minutes. Usually, if there's a heart problem, people might feel discomfort or pain, but he didn't mention anything that morning. I see Papa's passing as that of a highly virtuous soul leaving the body as Maha-Punya-Atma.

More than 60 years of my parents' togetherness ended on this day. Few years back they celebrated their 50th wedding anniversary. It was a more devastating for my mother than me.

Fig 3. 50th marriage anniversary of my parents

Early life and education

There is a small village called "Budhama" approximately 250 km east of Patna, capital of Bihar. The population of Budhama is about 1800-2000 (400-500 families, 2023). The village didn't have a proper road connecting it to thc nearest town (Saharasa or Madhepura).The nearest railways station is Saharasa (50 km). Prior to 1980, the village experienced a flood every year and cut it off from the rest of the state for months. The village also got its first electricity pole after 1990. One can imagine the poor condition of the area.

> *"As a child in the 1980s, we used to travel to our ancestral home in Budhama via a bullock or a horse cart from the nearest bus stop which was 5-6 km away. There were no proper roads; literally, our path was through the fields. I always liked to sit in the front side to see how the horse's tail were shaking back and forth while running in the field.*

Fig. 03 Location of village Budhama

My lineage is rooted in this village, as it was Dada ji 's (my grandfather) hometown. Dada Ji (Shri Dwarika Prasad) spent his entire life there since his childhood in that village. One day, I was curious about my lineage, great grandfathers and family history. Papa told me an interesting story.

Dada ji migrated/fled when he was very young, perhaps 7-8 years old, along with his elder brother and mother from another village in Bihar. My great grandfather was allegedly poisoned or killed during a work related travel. My great grandfather was an educated and well known man working as a Munsi (Munsi is an old profession who use to do accounting). This included collecting money for rich people, generally called a Zamindar in those days with several acres of lands. The family was more than financially stable. However, following his death, the financial situation deteriorated and faced several difficulties due to the British rule. They fled and left behind whatever they had. Dada ji's aunt (Fua) and Uncle (Fufa ji) who were living in the village Budhama took them in. Uncle of my grandfather was very rich and had hundreds of acres of agricultural lands. Later when my grandfather was grown up and got married at very early age of 16 years, so at early age he had several responsiblities, therefore, he started doing work for his uncle (such as taking care of his crops initially). Dada ji studied himself in order to get a job in the future so he can provide support for his family. He also started to take care of the land, account and collect money for his uncle. In return, he got few kg of rice or other grains per acre lands in a year, it was not a fixed per month. Hence, the financial and economic situation in the family remained poor and challenging.

My papa told me that most of the days, they were mainly eating roti of maize flour with potatoes, wheat flour and rice was like a feast once a while. My Dadi Ji (Smt Leeva Devi) was saved rice that he received in return of his work, and sell them to support the family and saved some money. By saving this way over several years, they were able to buy their own acres of agricultural lands in the same village but not many acres.

Fig 05 My grandfather (Sh. Dwarika Prasad) and grandmother (Smt. Leela Devi)

In Budhama, the majority of people lived in poverty, only few families called 'Zaminder' were rich and most of them were working for those rich people. Even though we had some land, given the location in the flood-prone Koshi region, crops were often destroyed by floods, making farming unprofitable. Every year due to the flood our house and crops were destroyed. Crops and vegetables grown in our fields were used to feed our family and served as a product for buying other groceries Therefore destruction by flood had devastating effects on them for several months, and getting a meal twice a day was a challenge. Buying grains and groceries in exchange of grains in those days were common, today we can't think about such type of tradition.

My dada ji was very kindhearted and a supportive person in the village. Despite of being poor, he was always willing to poor people in the village as much as he could.

He built a well in our land keeping in mind the poor people also have free access for water to the well;

Fig 6. Old well in the house in ancestral village which is no longer in use

"The walls of our home and most of the houses in the village were beautifully constructed with clay. It may be a sign of a poor family, but it was amazing how ecofriendly people were in past times. We were mostly visiting our village in the winter, the beds were made of several layers of dried paddy plant (dried material after harvesting) on the ground. It was a quite a skill to make a bed to sleep warm during the nights. Dada ji was very fond of making them for us. Normally the blankets were used to cover, but as a child I used to enter in-between the puaal during when trying to sleep. Even the roofs of the houses were made of those post harvested paddy plants materials (called as Puaal).

"We had a water well in the back of our ancestral house, the location was there so that poor families around our house could have free access to the

well for the water". The water of the well was very sweet. I liked to play and take bath on the well. The remanant of well is still there (see in the picture).

Fig 7. Ancestral village house in Budhama

Slowly things changed over years, due to a dam build by the government, floods reduced and famers were able to grow crops that they can use for meals and sell to buy food. The primary crop grown was paddy. My grandmother would process paddy into rice and store it for the entire year in a clay made container (called a kothi, which is a big container that opens from the top and also from the lower side to pick the grain from time to time) and used rice to exchange for other food items with villagers or shops. She used to make flattened rice (Chhura) with rice. When we had rice grown in our field, they were slightly better off and moved to daily meals (breakfast and lunch were mainly Dahi and Chhura), hence my Papa's favourite meal was Dahi and Chhura.

"My grandmother was a highly skilled lady, renowned for making exceptionally sweet and creamy yogurt (Dahi). Since we had a cow, she would typically prepare it using the milk from our cow. She would

heat the milk in a clay pot over a wooden fire until its volume reduced by half. Afterwards, she would transfer it to another clay pot, hanging it from the roof of the house overnight."

Papa was born in the same village in 1943, a few years before India's independence. All together Papa had seven siblings. Papa was the eldest son in the family and second oldest child after my aunt (Badi fua). Papa was born after my badi (eldest or big but in this context it is the former) fua (Aunt) however, between besides them 2 other sisters were born and died unexpectedly. Only the six of them were alive.

Being able to go to school in the 1950s and 1960s wasn't possible for most. The literacy rate of adults in Bihar was around only 13.49%. It required a lot of effort, time, perseverance, and dedication to enter into education. Dada Ji was a visionary who recognized education as the most important part of one's life. This vision was evident as all six of his children—three sons and three daughters (there were also two other daughters but like I stated before, they both died at a very young age) —received a secondary education.

Dada ji ensured that Papa received a proper education as the village didn't have primary and secondary school in those days. Because, my papa was like a prince for my Badi Fua. She loved him so much that even after her marriage to another village, she and her husband (Bade Fufa) took him to their home at age of 4-5 years. Papa did his initial studies while living with his eldest sister. They had a strong bond. After few years, papa came back to the village as my Dadi Ji (Being his Maa) also missed him. Since there wasn't a single school, he has to walk 2-3 km every day to attend primary and secondary schools in another village. Dada ji generally didn't receive any complaints from villagers or teachers. Papa was by nature a kind and sincere student. In this way papa completed his primary and secondary education.

Papa faced tremendous challenges to get his education. He had a choice to give up and work as a farmer and do agriculture, but despite of the difficulties, he made every effort to study and complete his education. He didn't just study Papa also started teaching young children to earn some money and support Dada ji. Dada ji's financial conditions were still bad. Agricultural produce still wasn't the best way to support a family of six. Papa was not only supporting himself but also saving his money to eventually help Dada ji.

After all of his struggles to get a better education, he succeeded and passed his middle school board exam in 1959. Because there was no school nearby to study further, he went back to his sister's home to his intermediate from MPHS (called as multiple purpose secondary school at that time) in Madhepura. As per our knowledge, there were only 2 students that managed to pass in the entire area.

It was very common in the past of our society to get married at an early age. While Papa studied to graduate, he stayed in Begusarai, a town far from his native place to do his BA degree and because that was the closest college in that region. He got married with my mother during his study in Begusarai. My maternal grandfather (Shri Harishankar Prasad) was from a village named Baghi in Begusarai. He was educated and worked as a typist in the Railway Divisional Office in Sonpur and had been living with his whole family in Sonpur. They lived in rented rooms belonging to a house.

Fig 8. An early days rare photo of Papa and Amma after marriage

At the time of their wedding Papa was only 19 years old and Amma was 16 years old. Amma had already completed her 10th board exam and passed in the 1st class. She quickly got a job as a teacher in a school in the village. There were only 2 female teachers in the school including her. Amma is a very important link as how Sonpur became karma Bhoomi (land of action) for Papa.

Papa continued his studies to complete his BA degree, however the responsibilities have grown because of marriage. Amma was a very sincere and serious student. She already started working as a teacher but also wanted to study further. So, at the very young age of 16 & 19, my parents took the responsibilities of the family of both sides. Amma was the eldest child among 10 siblings of my maternal grandfather - 7 sisters and 3 brothers. The financial conditions weren't good for nana ji's side.

Amma remembers that there were days when they were eating only one meal a day or if we were lucky 2 times. But it was always rice, dal and massed potato (Chhokha).

The very first step both made was to bear responsibility for their siblings (brothers and sisters). Taking it a step further, both personally took on the role of teaching each of their siblings and supporting their families financially by doing extra work such as giving tuition to children in the village.

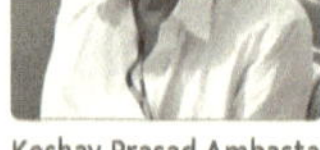

Keshav Prasad Ambasta Madan Mohan Prasad Ramchandra Prasad

Fig 9 Papa with his brothers

As per memory from my parents, the salary of Papa was Rs. 60 and mothers was Rs. 40, but it wasn't enough to support such a large family during the first few years of their job as a teacher.

An interesting story heard from my papa

There was an interesting tradition during the wedding to hold a competitive trivia debate the between groom's and bride's side. Educated people were needed for this debate so whenever a wedding happened my father - being an educated person - was always invited to be present in the marriage for such debate.

Once sindoordaan (a ritual that solemnizes the wedding) was finished. The next ritual to take place is called "Ghonta" where the groom's side of the family gifts jewelries and clothes to the bride. After this ritual, the debate starts between the two parties. A person of our village who was studying in a big city was called to participate for our side (we are the bride's side). When it was our turn, that person was asked to reply and ask a question to the groom's side. The person remembered an essay on "Flood", so he took the microphone and started speaking about Flood in full pace. Everyone was amazed to hear those in English. At the end of his essay, he stopped for 2 min, it was dead silent. No one understood what he said in English, but it was very clear to all that it was a very high advanced reply in English and the questions were also too difficult to answer. The groom's side couldn't understand. So, we won the game. Everyone was clapping.

About his personality

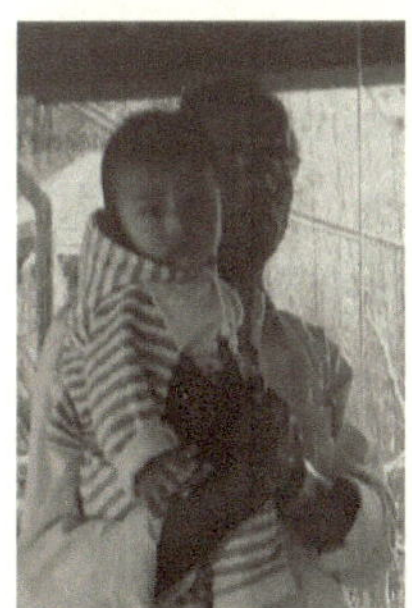

Papa lived a very simple life, he was down-to-earth and humble with high moral values. Papa was very calm and friendly. Even in tough situations, he remained calm and didn't get angry. He believed in solving problems by talking and understanding each other, not by fighting.

When I was studying in the 10th grade in Delhi, Papa told me not to show off or lie to your friends that your father is a principal, and we are a rich family in Bihar. Actually, he rightly picked a signal from my behavior and activities (sic). He didn't believe in bragging.

He had a soft and kind heart. He didn't hold grudges against anyone. His way of dealing with things is a good example of how to live a happy life by being friendly and not letting anger or arguments spoil things. In a world where people sometimes don't get along, Papa's way of being peaceful and friendly stands out as a great way to live a good life.

"Sir ji got angry very rarely, but whenever he got it only made you smile and laugh, he used to say one word "Bhusgol, kaam dhandha kuch nahi futani lamba chaura kaam chor", which words I still remember. But even at his anger, we used to smile and laugh." – Rakesh Raj Singh

In my interaction with hundreds of people who have known or worked with Papa, I never heard a single negative thing about him. A very surprising statement from many people was "he loved me/us or our family the most". It means that he made everyone felt important and loved, which is a very kind thing.

"You have never seen him get angry or saying this in a sweet Maithili language that makes you smile even at his anger" – Shri Ajit Kumar Sinha.

"He used to inspire everyone from home, family to society, town's children and girls. He always encouraged young women and youth for education and continued donating education till the last moment of his life" – Shri Hemchandra Verma

At the age of 23 years, Papa became the headmaster for the girls middle school Paharichak Sonpur. His dedication and honesty to teaching quickly made him well known in the village and nearby schools. His subject of teaching was Hindi, English and Sanskrit. Additionally, to further support the family, he was also working to give tuitions to the children in the villages.

In one incident that I remember well, once papa took me to lady's hut which was in our neighborhood in Budhama. She was an old poor lady living alone in a small hut made of bamboo sticks. She was sitting on the floor, along a small clay made cooking place, there was hardly anything in that hut. My papa and dada ji used to help her time to time. Papa asked me to touch her feet and take her blessings. I was young around 12 years old and bit hesitant to do so, but I followed as he said.

Later I asked why she was so important that you took me to her. There was a strong message in this gesture in my life that he taught me that day. So, he said that we should respect and help poor people, their blessings are very powerful. He also recalled a past incident that he didn't had a watch during his school and college days, he was asking my dada ji he could buy a watch because it is difficult sometime to reach in time and have to ask people the time for his activities, such as was also giving private tuitions and studying in a college. But, our family was not in condition to buy a watch in those times. That lady was sitting in house during that conversion and she said "one day you will be so capable that you can buy not one but many watches". Indeed, several years later, her words proved true.

This was purely coincidental that Papa got married into a family with similar views on education to all. With both my parents being teachers—Amma as the eldest of 10 siblings and Papa as the eldest son with four younger siblings—they jointly decided to make education the top priority for both sides of the family. As a result of their commitment, all of them achieved at least a college level of education (intermediate in those days), and many, particularly the women in our family, went on to become teachers in Bihar government schools.

Education definitely brings prosperity and progress in family. Our financial condition improved over the years. Progressive thinking resulted into improved quality of life over years and inspired the next generation to aim higher.

"Today, I am a director in a company, the most trusted person for my company owner because of bade papa. His living with honesty and integrity inspired me since my childhood and I imbibed those characters inside me. His motivation and help to get me a small job in Delhi

opened my career prospects." Maninder Kumar Sinha (Sanjay bhaiya), Jaipur

In the village and among his work friends, many preferred to have him with them for marriage talks, especially when it was about their daughters. They thought he was really good at talking and negotiating with the groom's family. In weddings in villages or to relatives, he acted like a guardian, always ready to solve problems between the families of the bride and groom, no matter which side he was on.

> *"He didn't only help in the field of education. Rather, he actively participated in social, matrimonial and social reform programs. He contributed to the development of marriageable boys and girls of countless families and communities". Shri Ajit Kumar Sinha (Bade Mama)*

One reason for why he was so good at negotiating was because he was an excellent listener. He would patiently listen to what others said before speaking. He never got upset by irrelevant topics, so he would reply calmly after thinking about the situation. That's why people always trusted him and asked for his help

He had an amazing sense of humor, especially with small children. My son, Yash, told me that he learned from Dada Ji how to play Ludo or any game with humor and in a funny way, not taking winning or losing too seriously.

When my nephew (Shantanu alias Janu) was only 6 years old, my sister was appearing for an exam in Patna. My nephew started crying upon seeing his mother, so Papa took him around Patna, showing him several places to distract him from crying.

An Ideal teacher - Sonpur his Karm-bhoomi

Fig 10. Papa with teacher colleagues of his school

Sonpur: Sonpur has been famous for two things in the past: 1) animal fairs (considered the largest animal fair in the word) when all animals including elephants, camels, and horses to birds were available for sale and 2) longest railway platform till 1990. It is beautifully located on the bank of 2 holy rivers Ganga and Gandak intersection in the Chapra (Saran) district of Bihar, 25 km from Patna airport. Another very important identification of Sonpur is loclation of Hindu Temple "Hari-Har" a beautiful temple where both Shiv and Vishnu bother in garvgrih are worshipped. Because of this temple, it is also called Harihar shretra.

Papa's life story is incomplete without mentioning Amma. Amma was also one of few girls who passed the 10th class in 1962 and joined as a teacher in the same school. My nana ji (Shri Harishankar Prasad -- maternal grandfather) was an equal visionary, ensuring education for all his children, regardless of gender. Amma, being the eldest among her 10 siblings, was exceptionally dedicated to her studies. She was one of the few girls in the district to reach this educational level at a time when the literacy rate for girls in Bihar was only 5% in 1951.

Fig 10a. My maternal grandfather (Shri Harishankar Prasad) & grandmother (Smt. Daya Devi)

After completion of Papa's education, Sonpur became his Karmabhomi. He started his first job as a teacher in Jang Bahadur School (currently known as Govt Middle School, Paharichak, Sonpur). Papa tried several places to work as a teacher. He got a temporary position in the school where Amma was a teacher, alredy married to Amma. Later, Papa got selected for the position of headmaster in the same school in Sonepur, as it was requirement of having a BA degree for the position of headmaster. Being a BA degree holder or a graduate was not very common in 1960s.

His life is a testament to the transformative power of education, the firm commit to his students, and a legacy built on principles of compassion, honesty, integrity, and dedication. He was a very disciplined teacher, in fact he was appointed directly as headmaster, meaning he had responsibility of both the school and teaching both. He was very punctual and also left as last. During his teure of 37 years as a headmaster, he served in 3 middle government schools. His school was always famous to have highest number of students enrolled and attendance and good quality of education. Papa focused on quality of teaching and ensured that teaching is conducted with scheduled timetable, that was not a normal things in most of schools.

Amma has made a huge contribution to Papa's life. Without her support and consent, Papa's time he gave to the society would not have been possible. Amma used to constantly help Papa in his work. What could be a greater example of their consent than the fact that my elder aunt (Mrs. Rita Sinha - Munna Mausi), her husband passed away shortly after their marriage, lived with us and got her education. She got enrolled in a teacher training school. Due to which she got a job as a teacher in a government school and became self-reliant. In those days, women had to face a lot of problems in the society after the death of their husbands. Second marriage was not respected in the society and they had to live at the mercy of their family members. Aunty was like a mother to me, she loved me a lot and nurtured me like a mother.

My mother's handwriting was very beautiful, just like pearls. I have often seen Amma doing writing related work which Papa used to give her to do. Amma was also very serious about the quality of teaching. She used to do all the classes in her school with great preparation. At home, it was mainly my mother who taught all of us brothers and sisters every day. I especially got punishment because I didn't pay attention to to the studies being like my sisters. An example of Amma's devotion towards education is that even today, at the age of 77, 3-4 children from the village, student of calss 5-10 class, come to study every day. She continued this even after Papa's death and she is very kind to those children. She often express worries what will happen to them if they do not study properly. I often see them explaining to children and scolding them lovingly.

In his schools, when teachers and students saw him entering the gate of school, everyone quickly dispersed and entered classroom. Papa was not a strict teacher but he was a role model and enforced that fellow teachers follow the rules. Only then can we teach students correctly.

> *In one of incidents he quoted "Once he asked a teacher to teach English to 7th standard students. That teacher was not very comfortable teaching English. Papa when he was not teaching class, was usually taking rounds around the school to go to the classroom to assess the teaching quality and for any other issues in classrooms. While this teacher was teaching class, papa realized that she was not giving the English lesson correctly. So, later he asked*

her and understood her problem with English and thereafter assigned it to another competent teacher."

My papa believed in all round development of students, so he was not only limited to studies, but he ensured extracurricular activities, for example, sports activities, events and celebrations. His school had organized one of the best Sarawati Pooja for several years in Kharika School, which I also attended. My papa's school were mostly 4-5 km away from home, he either rode a bicycle or walked to school.

Fig 11. Photo of Munna mausi (maternal aunt) with Amma (my mother)

Dedication and innovative teaching style are the hallmark of an ideal teacher. His style was also a new in those days. He was teaching subjects were languages such as English, Hindi and Sanskrit in schools. Guru-shishya parmpara was more prominent and normal for society in those days. Usually, parents hand over their children to the teachers to take care of study matter keeping in mind a better future of the student. Back in those days, it was common for teachers to be strict and use punishments, and students were often scared of them. But my papa was different. In a time when teachers were seen as terrifying, he made sure his classrooms were a friendly and comfortable places. He wanted students to feel at ease asking questions without being afraid.

Unlike other teachers, he never got angry or punished students. Instead, he built trust and confidence over the years. He made learning easy by using interesting examples and repeating them until everyone understood. He knew how to help students who found things difficult. Many students say they never saw him getting angery. He had his own special way of teaching that was kind and understanding. This type of behavior was amalgamated with his easy teaching styles. He recognizes a weak student is and knew how to handle them.

> *"Many people after doing 6 hours of duty as government school teacher remain confined to their family. But our Mausa Ji was not like that at all. While in government service, he used to spend time in social work, in public welfare or among educational activities and official works" Ashwani Kumar (Monu)*

> *"Keshav Sir was a very famous teacher of our area Sonpur. He was the favorite teacher of every house in our village as well as in the entire Sonpur, that is why every parent had the heartfelt desire that*

Keshav Sir should teach their child, which would prove useful in making their future bright. When we made mistakes, he used to explain to us lovingly. He used to guide us from time to time to move forward". Rakesh Raj Singh (ex-Student)

When I was in school in Delhi from 1991 to 1993, I consistently received the highest marks in Hindi and English subjects. My teachers were amazed by the quality of my writing in these languages. My teachers were surprised by my excellent knowledge in Hindi and English until they learned that I come from a family of teachers. During the two months of my summer vacation at home in Sonpur, Papa used to teach me the entire English and Hindi courses for the upcoming year. Thanks to his teaching, I could understand and remember everything for the entire year *His teaching is core of my English knowledge that helped me in higher studies and in English speaking foreign countries (Australia, USA, UK).*

His daily routine started early in the morning and continued until late in the evening, dedicated to teaching students. Retirement at the age of 60 did not signify an end to his service; instead, it marked the beginning of a new chapter. For another two decades, he continued to teach, mentor, guide, and support, leaving an indelible mark on the lives of successive generations. Headmaster, teachers, students and principal of several schools including girls high schools of the village are testament of his contribution in last 2 decades.

Achievements of his life

Girls education and women empowerment

> *"As an estimation, more than 50 female students became teachers in government school due him, single handedly and consistently supporting them throughout their career".*

He cared a lot about making sure girls had the same opportunities as boys to go to school. He believed that when girls get an education, it not only helps their families but the whole society. He worked incredibly hard to make sure that girls had equal opportunities for education. In a society where boys and girls were not treated equally, he worked very passionately to support girls' education. He firmly believed that empowering women through education was the key to social progress.

Back in 1970 and 1980 in Bihar, the literacy rate for girls were very low (approx 8-10%), not many girls were going to school. There were social barriers and early marriages that made it tough for girls to attend school. Papa was determined to help, motivate, and support girls and their parents.

> *"In those times girls used to only cook food and work at home, he taught me and got me admission*

in teaching training college. As a result, I got a job as a teacher in 1975. Being an educated mother, I taught my 2 sons and 1 daughter myself. After the sudden demise of my husband, my job kept my life and family economically sustainable, otherwise, we would've all lived on the streets" – Smt Asha Sinha, Retired School Teacher.

Fig. 12 Papa with his teachers to who he also taught them as a student

He went a step further and gave private lessons to women in the evening, right at their homes and in front of their families. Some even came to our home with lanterns because there was no electricity. His teaching style was excellent and trustworthy. People trusted him so much that they brought their daughters and wives to learn from him. They saw him as a reliable person, and that's why they had so much faith in him.

"I used to come in evening to take lessons from Sir, as in daytime I was not allowed to go outside of the home. He did all paperwork so that I could appear 10th board as a private candidate. Because of him, I later got admission in teacher training college, and as a result selected for government teacher job later on" Anonymous female student.

Women empowerment was not just a buzzword for Papa. He truly believed in the saying "Charity begins at home," and he lived by it. Amma was a teacher, having joined three years before Papa. She was already a living example of girls' education and a working woman in our family. In his time, both Papa and Amma made sure that all of my maternal aunts (mausi) and my paternal aunt (fua) received an education and became financially independent. As a result, three of my aunts and one paternal aunt, along with some uncles, became teachers and joined government schools. One of my uncles also became a teacher after finishing his studies.

He recognized the transformative power of education in uplifting the status of women and breaking the chains of societal constraints. By instilling a sense of confidence, independence, and ambition in his female students, he sowed the seeds for a future where women could actively participate in and contribute to all spheres of life.

"I am from a very poor family. I got married at a very young age and after having two children, my husband died suddenly. I came to my mother's place in Sonpur. On my mother's request, Master Saheb made me study in class 10. On the basis of which, with great effort, he helped me a lot in getting a job

as a maid in Anganwadi. Without his help, this poor and weak person would not have been able to do his job. Today I am standing on my feet after raising my two children and getting them educated." Smt Indu Devi, Anganwadi worker.

Fig 13. Smt Indu Devi with Amma

In those years, before the arrival of the internet and technology, most of the paperwork was done manually. Things like getting the 10th class board form, filling it out by hand, submitting it to the district office, collecting admit cards, and appearing for exams were all done through manual processes. Attesting certificates for job applications was a challenging task. Securing admission to a teacher training school and getting appointments from the education department in Patna required many steps and continuous efforts, often involving multiple visits to those offices in person.

For a girl and her parents who didn't know all the details of the process, it was almost impossible to navigate and appear for the 10th board exam, get admission to a teacher training school, and secure a job as a government teacher. During such challenging times, he personally took interest and provided help at every step of the entire process—from education to board exams, admission to teacher training school, to appointment at the school. He visited the education department in both the district office and capital Patna numerous times over the years, and many officials knew him for his goodwill and dedication. For 30-40 years, every single year, he tirelessly provided this kind of help and support to numerous students.

He helped anyone without any discrimination who came to him for his help and support. All these additional activities kept occupied him since morning to late in evening, in addition to the teaching. He never made any distinction between his own family and others.

> *"For him, the boundaries of his family were very large, whoever comes to him, he was treating and helping them as his own family member. Very often, we have seen people (teachers, parents, students) started coming to our home very early to meet "master saab or sir", around 5 am for teaching related works." "Smt Alpna Sinha (Deji didi) and Smt Rashmi Sinha (didi - sister).*

He believed that education could make a big difference in one's lives, helping them break free from the limit of society. He encouraged his female students to be confident, independent, and ambitious. He wanted them to have a bright future where they could take part in everything life has to offer. In our community, we've seen how things change when women get good jobs, like being teachers or working for the government. Their families become financially stable, and their kids get a good education.

Even those who chose to stay at home made a positive impact. They understood the importance of education and helped their kids learn. So, thanks to my Papa's efforts, lots of families have changed for the better, becoming stronger, more educated, and financially stable.

Professional life

During a certain period, he managed the salary and payment processing for teachers in middle schools across three blocks (tahsil). In those years, the headmaster was responsible for preparing the teachers' salaries and submitting them to the treasury. Due to a lack of headmasters in several schools, he worked single-handedly to compile salary data for more than a 100 teachers in those schools.

His professional life comprised various facets. He served as the president of Prathmik Shikshak Sangh for several years. Additionally, he actively participated in extracurricular activities involving students, such as scouting and guiding, musical events, and the celebration of school functions.

In a noteworthy event, around the age of 72, villagers requested him to organize the annual Durga Pooja event, appointing him as the treasurer. It turned out to be one of the most memorable events as people trusted him, resulting in significant donations. After all expenses, he managed to save around 2 lakh rupees, which was utilized in the following year.

Post-Retirement life

Fig 14. Retirement function at Barbatta School, Sonpur (2002)

There are only a few people who after retirement are actively connected with their profession. Education is such a profession and Papa too kept connected. However, his commitment to education knew no bounds. Retirement marked a new chapter in his life, one where he continued to serve as a guiding force for the third and fourth generations. His passion for education remained undiminished, and he found innovative ways to contribute to the learning process.

Even 20 years post-retirement, he was as much connected with students and teachers of several schools and actively involved in teaching, guiding and mentoring and supporting educational activities. Most retired teachers aren't remembered by schools after such a long time, but Papa was. He was well known amongst 10th students appearing for board exam even in 2023.

> *"Even after retirement, he was continuously engaged in studies. Whatever teachers of our Pahadichak Girls School faced any problem, they always remembered him. His personal experience was so wide that everyone approached him for advice."*

During this 20 years post-retirement, he was still connected to students and their parents appearing for 10th exams in 2022 or 2023, those were coming to our home along with their parent for filling of forms or guidance.

Often, he got phone calls of headmaster or teachers of several schools in nearby for his expertise on retirements and pensions related matters of teachers.

> *"Whenever I called him from Belgium during the day, he was usually in a high school. I asked him why he didn't rest more at home, and he politely said, "I feel better sitting at the school than at home." – Dr. Gaurav Kumar (Son)*

Even in his eighties, Papa's energy and enthusiasm for educational pursuits were unparalleled. His daily routine involved not just personal reflection but active engagement in educational activities. Whether it was assisting with admissions, providing coaching, or overseeing the educational works of schools, he remained an indispensable asset to the community. His enduring commitment to education was a testament to the fact that teaching, for him, was not just a profession but a lifelong vocation.

Lived a healthy life

He is like a guide for how to be healthy, and I've learned a lot from him. He showed me by the way he lives, his morning routine started from 5 am by doing Yoga everyday, and morning walk, bath and pooja before his breakfast and leaving home for his work.

> *"I remember that once, in 1997 at the age of 44, he had a slight problem with his heart. Instead of ignoring it, he made some big changes in his life. He stopped riding his motorcycle and started using his bicycle every day like he used to. In fact, he sold the motorcycle only for his health reason. He was cycling a lot, sometimes up to 10-15 kilometers every day till his last day. He also started getting regular health check-ups and blood tests, not waiting for something bad to happen."*

At the age of 80, when he found cycling to be getting more challenging, he suggested that I buy him an electric bicycle. In November 2022, I got him one, and he was thrilled to use it every day. He once mentioned to me, "Wherever I go, people gather around to see the electric bicycle."

His way of taking care of himself is not just for him; it's like a gift he's given to our whole family. It's a lesson in being healthy and taking care of ourselves that goes beyond just what we do at home.

Parenting Perspectives: Guidance for Effective Teaching

My parents never imposed a specific career path on me; instead, they allowed me the freedom to choose my own academic journey. At the age of 12, they sent me to live with my maternal uncle in Delhi to access better educational opportunities. My bade mama (Maternal uncle - Sh. Ajit Kumar Sinha) was my guardian. He took care of my education. Many of my traits is inspired from his ethical and moral values in his life. I worked diligently and consistently excelled in my exams. Initially aspiring to become a medical doctor, I encountered challenges in qualifying after a few attempts. It was during this time that I discovered the field of pharmacy.

Under the University of Delhi, I secured admission to a reputed pharmacy college in the diploma stream based on merit. During my diploma studies, I developed a keen interest in pursuing further education in pharmacy with aspirations of becoming a scientist. Subsequently, I pursued a B.Pharma degree and qualified for the GATE exam with a percentile of 97.3, earning admission to Panjab University, Chandigarh, with a scholarship. Throughout this educational journey, Papa consistently supported me, encouraging me to apply for positions in the government sector, particularly as a pharmacist.

Fortuitously, I qualified in the written exam for the Railway Pharmacist position but faced an unsuccessful interview. Following the completion of my master's degree, I secured a position as a lecturer in the Department of Pharmacy at a reputable government institute in Indore in 2003. Papa celebrated this achievement, acknowledging that I had surpassed his own career progression and comparing my starting pay scale favorably to his at retirement.

Fig 15. At the time of joining as a lecturer (2004)

Despite my professional success, I harbored a desire to pursue a career as a scientist, aiming for research and a Ph.D. I was determined to undertake this journey abroad at a prestigious university. Fortunately, I found an opportunity in Australia. While Papa was delighted with my accomplishments, he hesitated to endorse my decision to resign from my lecturer position.

During my own educational journey, I joined as a lecturer in the Department of Pharmacy in 2003 without prior knowledge of how to prepare or conduct classes.

I began by using pharmacology books, teaching while referencing texts and writing on the blackboard. When Papa inquired about my lecture preparation, I mentioned relying on the book. In response, he provided valuable tips on effective preparation, student engagement, and creating an interesting classroom environment. As a result, my teaching became highly effective, with several students choosing to specialize in pharmacology. Some have gone on to become leading scientists in top institutes in Australia, the US, and the UK.

Concluding remark:

As his son, I feel an inherent responsibility to immortalize his life's work through a book. This endeavor goes beyond a mere recounting of events; it is a tribute to a great person who dedicated his entire life to a noble cause. The book aims to capture the essence of his teachings, the transformative moments in the lives of his students, women empowerment, and the societal changes he catalyzed through his unwavering commitment.

In crafting this narrative, I aspire to inspire future generations to recognize the profound impact a dedicated educator can have on society. Papa's life serves as a beacon, guiding us towards a future where education is not just a means to acquire knowledge but a catalyst for positive change, empowerment, and societal progress.

When I was in Australia during my Ph.D., I was thrilled to bring my parents to a foreign land. Somehow, he was convinced and obtained a visa. He boarded a flight, possibly Singapore or Malaysia Airlines (I don't remember exactly), traveling with my wife and a few months old son Yash to Melbourne. It was a remarkable journey. He explored Melbourne city on foot, walking several kilometers every day, keenly observing everything for several hours.

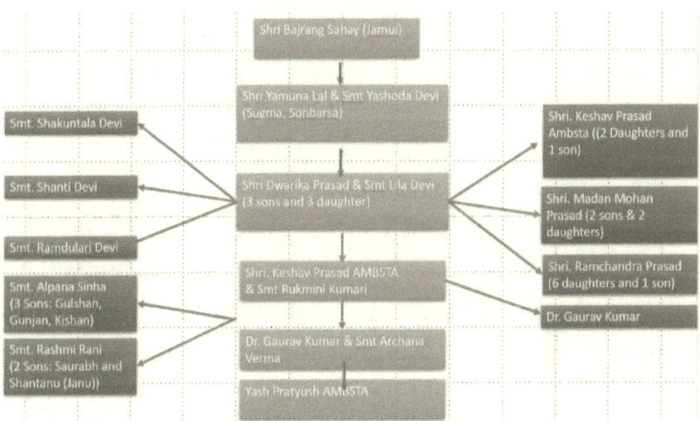

Fig 16. a) First flight and first foreign country visit landing on Melbourne airport along with my wife and few months old son Yash , b) Visiting "The Twelve Apostles" in Melbourne, c) family lineage

Later, when I moved to Belgium, I wanted him to visit here as well. He came in 2017. Since the official languages in Belgium are Dutch and French, and my son speaks Dutch, he started learning basic Dutch. Once again, he explored Antwerp on foot, discovering several places that we hadn't seen yet.

Acknowledgement

Through this book, I want to convey my deep emotional gratitude to everyone who supported me unconditionally and selflessly during this challenging time. In the following 15 days after Papa's death, I experienced overwhelming support from various quarters—family members, relatives, neighbors, villagers, teachers, his ex-colleagues, and friends. The past one year has been emotionally challenging for me, and I want to acknowledge and name a few individuals for their extraordinary emotional and physical support.

I genuinely believe that their support, coupled with the respect Papa had earned over the years, has been instrumental in my ability to stand strong today. I was not mentally prepared for the sudden loss of Papa. I have been living so confidently and free from any and all worries of my family in India that I never expected in my wildest dreams that this would happen to me so sudden. When I heard the news early in the morning my fingers got numbs, and my voice was chocked. Although I was trying to stay strong and holding my tears, after Vijay dropped me on airport, my tears were rolling continuously over my face during flights. The most difficult journey of my life was the last part after landing from Patna airport to reaching home, I couldn't to imagine how I would handle myself. After reaching, I cried my heart out hugging my Papa, however, soon I saw the conditions of Amma, sisters and relatives and how they were emotionally drenched, I didn't cry afterward in front of anyone.

I express my heartfelt thanks and gratitude to Deji Didi, Kamkam Didi, and Chhote Jija Ji. All three of them were so strongly holding Amma to give her hope of life. I was extremely worried if I may lose Amma given her deteriorating condition, as she has not taken a drop of water or food for several days. They were supporting me in daily rituals and emotionally supporting each other (3 strong emotional bonds). My wife Archana is a real companion in happiness and sorrow and understands what I need and how I think. It was extremely difficult for me living in Sonpur, after spending over 18 years in developed countries, but she understood and tried to make my condition well. She was a champion in taking care of my activities and responsibilities back in

Belgium alone (refection of a strong women). Chhote Papa (Shri. Madam Mohan Prasad), Bade Mama (Sh. Ajit Kuamr Sinha), Chhote Bhaiya (Sh. Hemchandra Verma, Madhepura) were 3 strong pillars of the family and for me. They never left me and my family alone for over 15-20 days. Until all rituals and related work at home were done, only then did they leave for their home. They were there for me at every moment of my need. Manoj Mama and Sanjay Bhaiya were like 2 gems of love and affection, their emotional attachment and care to me were unforgettable, in addition to supporting other things. Vijay has been my best friend for over 2 decades, I rely and trust him blindly. He was with me within a few minutes once I called him in early morning after I heard about my Papa's death. He came and took care of my immediate needs and emotional supports, as my brain was not working well after hearing such sudden news. Regarding my absence in Belgium for almost 2 months, I was completely stress free that is how much I trust him. Dhananjay Bhaiya (Shri Dhananjay Singh - my neighbor) was so concerned after my Papa's death, he really acted like a guardian and gave me so much loving care and support that I felt confident that I am not left alone in the village. Thanks to Shr. Ajay Kumar Singh (Nunnu bhaiya) for his unconditional support and help in oversighting rituals activities. Yash is too young but from his perspective, it was very comforting that he understood the situation, when he came here in Sonpur, he mingled well with the family and children, quickly adapted to crowdy home with 60-70 people, that I never felt worried from his perspective of that how he would cope this emotional situation. It was also a positive thing to my mental condition. All of these heroes of my life, their unwavering support at every step was so significant that I didn't feel the overwhelming pressure and stress during the first month and after. They were strong pillars in my life. I had never experienced such a strong bond in my family in this difficult time before.

All the last rites and rituals were conducted smoothly, and after the rituals, I was able to manage both my family in India and home in Belgium equally well.

I especially would like to thank to Chhote papa and Bade Mama for their constant discussion, writing and drafting of this book. They regularly provided me inputs and valuable information about my Papa's life. Their contribution in completion of this book is significant. Many thanks to Vijay and Yash for his review and edit of this book. Thanks to all who took time to write their experiences with Papa. Thank you to Gullu bhaiya (Mr. Rakesh Raj Singh) for his constant supporting me as an over last years as an elder brother in the village and Bantu (Simant Singh Gautam) for in preparation of this book. I also heartfelt thank to Umesh Thakur and maid Lalita's mother (smt Chinta Devi) for their day and night supports for all rituals and works at my home.

Experiences from family, relatives, students, teachers, and friends

Smt Asha Sinha (Asha Mausi) - Retired School Teacher, Chapra

Ashwani Kumar (Monu), Chapra – BPSC qualified 10-12th Class teacher in Government School, Chapra

"Mausa Ji". Whom we all fondly called Badka Mausa. He was not only elder in name. But he has also discharged all the responsibilities. There would hardly be anyone in whose life uncle ji has not played some important role. As my mother also says that in those times girls used to only cook the stove, in those times a bade mausa ji came to teach us in Sonpur. He was helpful in providing opportunity to read and write and got admission in teaching training college. As a result, I got a job as a teacher. Otherwise, today we all used to live on the streets. For Mausaji, the circle of family was very vast. Today, where people like to stay limited to a few, the same uncle, every relative and whoever was in contact with him was his family, used to be a part of it. There was not the slightest hesitation in being present in anyone's happiness and sorrow in every way. I myself have not had good relations with my cousins, friends and aunts, but today I am with them. We all have a good relationship. Mausaji has also played an important role in this positive change. In today's era, leave the money, even if any advice is asked on time, then most of the people will give wrong advice. Whereas Mausaji is great for everyone. Be it money, physical support, paper work, recommendation, or any advice, I have found him standing in every way. Whoever has distanced himself from him and has been at a loss, he was a storehouse of positive energy. I got the opportunity to visit Sonpur, Hajipur along with me. I have seen that there will hardly be anyone who does not know him. His specialty was to meet everyone lovingly, talk to them and listen to people carefully. No matter how big the problem was, he used to tell them casually, no problem, everything will be fine. When people start banging their heads when there is a big problem, uncle used to remain calm even at that time. Only in very special circumstances, he used to give process to someone's employees, otherwise he used to end the dispute peacefully. He always used to inspire people around him to resolve mutual disputes and bitterness. Educational and government appointment. Many people do the job of a government teacher, who after doing 6 hours of duty, come straight home and remain confined to their family. But our Mausa Ji was not like that at all. While in government service, he used to spend time in social work, in public worship or among official works. Even after retirement, he was always involved in teaching related work. The biggest quality of Mausaji was that he would always teach people for studies but would also inspire them for competitive exams. Nothing negative ever came out of his mouth. Once I had told my uncle that I will try to crack the competitive exams for two more years, whether I get a government job or not. On this, uncle ji said, no, don't say that and it won't be just in 2 years but you will get it within 2 years. Meanwhile, uncle ji passed away. I succeeded in many examinations. Within these one and a half years, I passed the teacher recruitment examination conducted by BPSC in the first attempt and was selected for classes XI and XII. Sadly, he is no more with us today, but uncle has been the source of inspiration for this happy outcome. Mausa ji dedicated his entire life to education, women's education and other social and public works. Even though you are not physically present among us today, we have learned from you and will always remain among us as guides.

Shri. Hem Chandra Verma - Retired District Office Superintendent, Bihar Govt (Chhote Bhaiya)

Controlling the uncontrolled energy of life and taking life in the right direction towards a healthy life, long life and successes, he used to inspire people to move ahead. And he used to inspire everyone from home, family to society, town's children and girls. He always encouraged young women and youth for education. He continued donating education till the last moment of his life. He was an ideal teacher as well as a very skilled and excellent parent. Due to his successful and efficient leadership, we always keep moving forward as per our karma. He studied fourth and fifth class from Primary School Tuniyahi, after that he completed his studies from MPHS Intermediate Inter Level Multipurpose Higher Secondary School Madhepura and completed his further studies from College Begusarai and other places. While studying in MahaVidyalaya in Begusarai, his marriage took place in Begusarai. As an organization officer of Education Department in Sonpur, he provided efficient leadership.

Smt Alpana Sinha, Teacher in Govt Middle School, Paharichak, Sonpur.

My parents, both Papa and mother, were committed to ensuring that I received a good education and excelled in my studies. When I passed my 10th grade with a first-class distinction, Papa encouraged me to prepare for competitive exams, especially medical. However, my inclination was to follow in Amma's footsteps and become a teacher. I chose to pursue teacher training, and completed BA. After a few years, I secured a government teaching job.

Papa consistently emphasized the importance of staying well-informed by reading newspapers and keeping up with general knowledge. He remained a constant support, helping me with any administrative work related to the school until his last moments.

On the final day, as I left for school at 9 am and forgot my water bottle, he kindly filled it and instructed the maid to send it to the school. His caring nature extended not only to me but to everyone around him.

Smt. Rashmi Rani, Teacher, Govt Middle School, Baghi, Begusarai.

Papa made sure that both my sister and I received an education like any other child. Both my parents were our teachers. I attended a school in the village, and Papa's life and routine were always inspiring to me. Papa wanted us to become doctor, that was also my dream. I worked hard and achieved first class with excellent marks in those days, but could not get into medical. He encouraged me do study further. Because of his encouragement and support, I completed Teacher training, BA and MA before my marriage.

Papa supported my decision to attend the teacher training school in another city. Though transportation was not very convenient, he helped me stay at the hostel of the training school. Throughout my training, he visited me and my friends, assisting with my studies and other requirements.

After completing the training, I was placed on a waiting list for a teaching position in government school as per rules in Bihar. When Papa learned that my joining might be delayed for a few years, he tried to convince me for preparation of competitive exams. It was challenging for me as I had significant responsibilities of two small children.

In the end, I secured a teaching position as a teacher in a government middle school in Begusarai. I taught my 2 children, one of them got a good job in public sector company (ONGC subsidiary) and other one is preparing for medical entrance exam. It was only because of Papa that we are living a good life.

"Shri Ajit Kumar Sinha (Retired Office superintendent, Northern Raily Head Office, Delhi

Today we are going to talk about a person who, using limited natural, family and social resources during his lifetime, provided unforgettable service to his family and society for about 60 years through his educational qualification, experience and hard work. He was our revered and respected "Keshav Babu", whom we knew as Badka Mehman in our family. He was fond of reading and teaching since childhood. After higher education in Begusarai, she created history in the field of education along with her elder sister (Mrs. Rukmini Kumari), who became her wonderful life partner. At a very young age, due to his reputation and ability, he became the headmaster of Jang Bahadur Singh Girls Secondary school, which is currently running smoothly under the name of Government Secondary Girls School, this school must have been the first girls middle school in Harihar area at that time. This school is unprecedented in women empowerment. He was the protector, guardian and guide not only of me but of all the members of my family. His advice was necessary in all the work at home. He was a man with a versatile personality.

His identity was not only in the field of education. Rather, he actively participated in social, matrimonial and social reform programs. He contributed in providing marriageable boys and girls to countless families and societies. You have never seen him getting angry or saying this in a sweet Maithili language that makes you smile even at his anger. Being a resident of Maithali region, his language Manhar was very melodious. He was very loving. His daily work start from 5:00 am to 10:00 pm, he used to perform yoga practice, puja, bath, food and teaching etc. exactly as per the time schedule. He was very fond of eating paan. By feeding him paan, you could hypnotize him towards you. His absence is an irreparable loss to our lives and family, his memory is unforgettable, with respect

Shri Rakesh Raj Singh (Gullu Bhaiya)

Our dear sir "Keshav Master saheb"

When parents give birth to us, teachers make us successful in life. Teachers play an important role in our lives. Along with studies, they also teach us the art of living. Teachers teach us and give us knowledge. They help us to become good citizens by teaching us, teachers make our future, teachers are given the status of God.

Although there are many teachers in my life and I like all of them very much, but among them all, my most favorite teacher was Sir of our village "Keshav Master Sahib", he was an ideal teacher.

Keshav sir was simple, calm and a winner by nature. His personality was very impressive but he was very punctual and well-liked. As beautiful and attractive as his outer personality was, his nature was equally good and sociable. He believed that we should have a positive attitude towards life. Our path Whatever challenge comes in his life, he should face it boldly. Discipline was of great importance in his life. He always gave us doubt to follow the right path. When we made mistakes, he used to explain us lovingly. He used to guide us to move forward from time to time. When Sir ji got very angry, he used to say one word "Bhusgol, Kam Dhandha Kuch Nahi Futani Lamba Chaura Kaam Chor", which words I still remember. But even at his anger, we used to smile and laugh.

Keshav Sir was a very famous teacher of our area Sonpur. He was the favorite teacher of every house in our village as well as in the entire Sonpur, that is why every parent had the heartfelt desire that Keshav Sir should teach their child, which would prove helpful in making their bright future.

All the children in our house took education from Sir ji for the last 40 years till now. In which my elder sister, sister, elder brother and my younger sister along with me got the privilege of studying from Sir ji. Whatever knowledge we have in the form of education today, the credit for its beginning goes to Keshav Sir. He had good knowledge of many subjects. He had very good knowledge of English language. His way of teaching was very simple. He also acted as a guide for us from time to time to move forward. Along with studies, he also taught us the art of living.

It was a year ago that Durga Puja was organized every year in our village. For which puja, a committee is formed by the entire village residents, in which once in 2017, a committee was formed under the leadership of Keshav Sir. Sirji was elected as the treasurer of that committee. I also got the opportunity to work as a member of that committee. Preparations for the puja started and with the blessings of Maa Durga everything went well and the puja was completed. Like every year, this time too after the puja was over, when the expenses were calculated, the highest amount of rupees (1,84,365) was saved, which till date in the history, no committee had saved that much money which was done by the Treasurer of Keshav Sir. I am very fortunate to have a teacher like Keshav Sir and I respect and honor his experience. I treat him like a God. Whatever I am today is because of my teacher.

Simant Singh Gautam (Bantu)

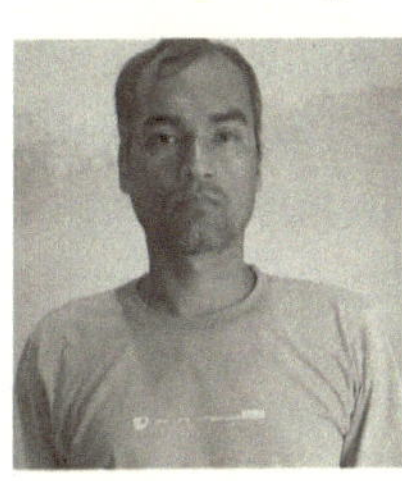

It is an eternal truth that the human being who has given birth on this earth is certain to die. His demise is my personal loss. I followed him from childhood till youth. I will continue to do so in future also. His entire life was like an open book which anyone could read easily. He gave the teaching profession such a great place that no one can ignore him. I always saw the enthusiasm and passion in him which showed that a person is a constant and continuously working creature.

Even after retirement, he was continuously engaged in studies. Whatever teachers of our Pahadichak Girls School faced any problem, they always remembered him. His personal experience was so wide that everyone approached him for advice. His biggest specialty was that he never worried, nor was he ever under stress. He did the teaching profession with full dedication and proves that it is only the work of a person that makes him great. I taught with him for many years and kept getting inspired by him. All the students in the class easily understood what he said. His friendly behavior with every class was the same. He had the same reputation in every class, which shows that he was very popular in all the classes, being influenced by him, I started teaching. I often took advice from him, which made him very happy.

It is very difficult to compensate for his death. His ideals will always remain with me and I will continue to take inspiration from him. Because of them, I also solve every problem with ease and simplicity. He made me patient so that I never felt any problem. He often used to say that get so engrossed in any work that it becomes your hobby, so that you can keep doing it. May you feel joy. Even today, I have assimilated his words throughout my life, due to which I never face any problem and perhaps I don't know what to write about his personality, the more I write, the less it is. His greatness will always inspire me.

Satya Prakash Singh (Nunnu, Paharichak, Sonpur)

Keshav Sir, I am deeply saddened by his untimely death. He never considered himself retired. He dedicated his entire life to the cause of education and teaching - be it any work related to education, he never said no to anyone. I myself was associated with him in teaching work for 14-15 years. I never saw him getting tired.

My attachment with him was very deep. He always remained a source of inspiration for me, who honed my teaching skills through his experience. Once, along with the youth, we also joined the Puja Committee (Durga Puja) and worked very enthusiastically and that year's Puja and donations were donated to our It was at its peak. My repeated thanks to such a great man,

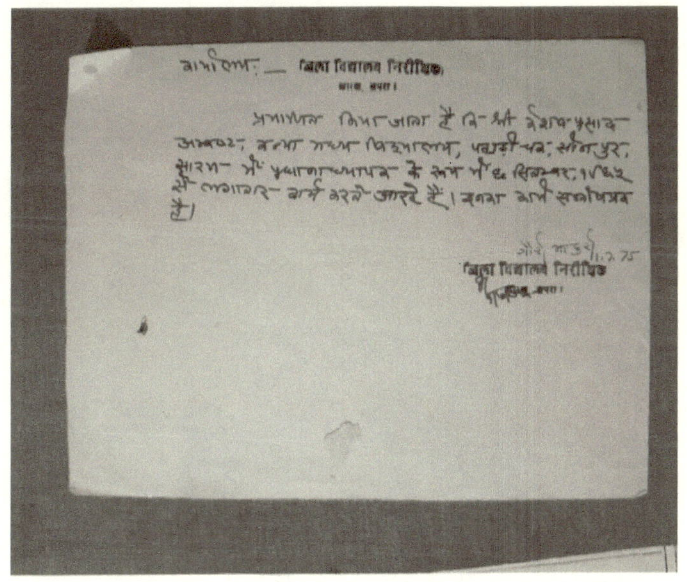

कार्यालय :— जिला विद्यालय निरीक्षक,
सारण, छपरा।

प्रमाणित किया जाता है कि श्री केशव प्रसाद अम्बष्ठ, कन्या मध्य विद्यालय, पचाढ़ी चक, सोनपुर, सारण में प्रधानाध्यापक के रूप में ६ सितम्बर, १९६२ से लगातार कार्य करते आ रहे हैं। इनका कार्य सन्तोषप्रद है।

1.2.75
जिला विद्यालय निरीक्षक
सारण, छपरा।

Part 2 हिंदी

Fig 2. यश (पोते) द्वारा अपने दादा जी को श्रद्धांजलि पोते ने बनाई दादाजी की पसंदीदा फूल (गेंदा)

पृष्ठभूमि/प्रस्तावना

हाल ही में, एक प्रमुख समाचार पत्र में दिल को छू लेने वाली एक शीर्षक ने मेरा ध्यान खींचा: "गुमनाम नायक: 20 पद्म श्री पुरस्कार विजेता जो अब तक अज्ञात बने हुए हैं।" मेरा विश्वास है की हमारे राज्य और देश में बहुत से व्यक्ति समाज की भलाई के लिए निस्वार्थ रूप से योगदान और समाज सेवा करते हैं। इन गुमनाम नायकों के बीच, मुझे विश्वास है कि मेरे पिता (पापा) एक उदाहरण हैं, जो निःस्वार्थ भाव से अपने आसपास के लोगों के जीवन पर शिक्षा के माध्यम से सकारात्मक प्रभाव एवं बदलाव लाने के लिए खुद को समर्पित किये| एक पिता, शिक्षक, गुरु, सामाजिक और मानवतावादी व्यक्ति की जीवनी, जिन्होंने ग्रामीण भारत में 21वीं सदी में सकारात्मक बदलाव लाने के लिए सामाजिक, नैतिक, शैक्षिक और महिला सशक्तिकरण सेवाओं के लिए अपना पूरा जीवन समर्पित कर दिया।

बिहार के एक सुदूर गांव में एक गरीब परिवार में जन्मे, उन्होंने शिक्षा प्राप्त करने के लिए संघर्ष किया, खुद को और परिवार को सशक्त बनाया और फिर शिक्षा से समाज के सैकड़ों लोगों का जीवन बदलने में सहभागी बने । वे बहुत ही अनुशासित और ईमानदार व्यक्ति एवं शिक्षक थे | एक प्रधानाध्यापक के रूप में अपने 37 वर्षों के कार्यकाल के दौरान अपनी नौकरी से कहीं अधिक कार्य किया। अपने छात्रों को शिक्षित कर के एक अच्छा इंसान बनाने और समाज में कैसे एक अच्छी जिंदगी जी सके इसके लिए बहुत गंभीरता से उसे संस्कारीत किए और जिम्मेदारियाँ को बखूबी निभाया| उन्होंने न केवल उन्हे संस्कारीत किया पढ़ाया बल्कि उनके परिवारों को प्रोत्साहित और मदद भी की। वह यह सुनिश्चित करने में विश्वास करते थे कि लड़कियों को अच्छी

शिक्षा मिले, खासकर जब 1970 के दशक में ग्रामीण इलाको में लड़कियों को शिक्षण देने के लिए आवश्यक नहीं समझा जाता था। यह उस समय की बात है जब साक्षरता दर कम थी (13%) और लैंगिक समानता के खिलाफ सामाजिक बाधाओं के कारण बिहार में लड़कियों को स्कूल जाने के लिए प्रोत्साहित नहीं किया जाता था।

2002 में 60 वर्ष की आयु में सेवानिवृत्त होने के बाद, मैंने उन्हें हमेशा अपने स्वास्थ्य, आहार, व्यायाम के प्रति सक्रिय और जागरूक देखा | जिस बात ने मुझे सबसे अधिक प्रभावित किया वह यह थी कि 80 वर्ष की आयु में भी वह कितने ऊर्जावान थे। वह नियमित रूप से बहुत पैदल चलते थे, यहां तक कि साइकिल भी चलाते थे। अक्सर वह प्रवेश, कोचिंग, शिक्षण, या स्कूल से संबंधित किसी भी अन्य प्रशासनिक कार्यों में स्कूल स्टाफ की मदद करते रहते थे । वह सिर्फ छात्रों के प्रति ही समर्पित नहीं थे; उन्होंने अन्य शिक्षकों को उनके रोजमर्रा के कामों में भी मदद की। वह यह सब 4 मार्च, 2023 को अपने अंतिम दिन तक करते रहे। जब भी हमारी बात होती थी तो वह मुझसे यही कहते थे कि वह हमारे गांव के गर्ल्स स्कूल में शिक्षा संबंधी कुछ कार्यों में व्यस्त हैं।

इतनी अधिक उम्र में उनकी जीवटता और प्रतिबद्धता एक मिसाल है । उनके बेटे के रूप में, मैं उनकी जीवनी के माध्यम से उनकी विरासत को अमर बनाने का कर्तव्य महसूस करता हूं, इस आशा के साथ की यह आने वाली पीढ़ियों के लिए एक श्रद्धांजलि और प्रेरणा के रूप में काम करेगा।

उनकी जीवन यात्रा का अवलोकन

1943: 1 जनवरी, 1943 को जन्म
1959: मिडिल स्कूल बोर्ड परीक्षा (मधेपुरा) उत्तीर्ण की
1963: मध्य विद्यालय, गांधी आश्रम, पहाड़ीचक, सोनपुर में अस्थायी शिक्षक के रूप में नियुक्त किये गये। (जंग बहादुर सिंह स्कूल के नाम से था तब)
1962: मेरी माँ श्रीमती रुक्मिणी कुमारी के साथ विवाह
1963: कला स्नातक (बीए) पूरा किये (जीडी कॉलेज, बेगुसराय, भागलपुर विश्वविद्यालय)
1965: मध्य विद्यालय, गांधी आश्रम, पहाड़ीचक, सोनपुर में प्रधानाध्यापक के रूप में कार्यभार ग्रहण किये ।
1980: राजनीति विज्ञान में मास्टर ऑफ आर्ट्स (एमए) बिहार विश्वविद्यालय) किये
1975: शिक्षण में डिप्लोमा (बिहारविश्व विद्यालय) किये
2002: 40 साल की सेवा के बाद सेवानिवृत्त हुए

उनका अंतिम दिन: 04 मार्च, 2023

इस जीवनी की शुरआत मैं उनके अंतिम दिन से शुरू करना चाहता हूँ 4 मार्च, 2023 का दिन था, जो मेरे जीवन में हमेशा के लिए एक अविस्मरणीय दिन बन गया । क्योंकि उनका निधन इतना शांतिपूर्ण तरीके से हुआ, जैसे किसी व्यक्ति ने अपने अंतिम दिन बिना किसी दर्द या पीड़ा का अनुभव किए गहन ध्यान या समाधि को प्राप्त की हो। वे बीमार नहीं थे और उन्हें किसी भी प्रकार की कोई गंभीर बीमारी नहीं थी। 80 साल की उम्र में भी वह सक्रिय और स्वस्थ थे।

वह शनिवार की सुबह थी वह सुबह 6 बजे उठकर अपनी दिनचर्या पूरा किये। अपनी सभी दैनिक कार्य और योग करने के बाद, उन्होंने स्नान किया और हमारी सबसे पवित्र धर्मिकग्रन्थ "श्री रामचरित मानस" पढ़ने के लिए तैयार हुए, जो कि वह पिछले 30 वर्षों से हर शनिवार को नियमित रूप से करते आ रहे थे ।

सुबह 9-10 बजे पुजा किये, उन्होंने लगभग 30-40 मिनट तक श्री रामचरित मानसपढ़ी, उसके बाद पवित्र शंख बजाया। पुजा के बाद, वह हाथ में धूपबत्ती लेकर पुजा से बाहर आये और उसे अम्मा (मेरी माँ - मैं अपनी माँ को अम्मा ही कह कर बुलाता हूँ) को धूपबत्ती पकड़ाया । जैसे ही वह धूपबत्ती रखने के लिए कमरे में गई, उसे कुछ आवाज सुनाई दी। जल्दी से वापस आकर उन्होंने देखा कि पापा बेहोश होकर फर्श पर पड़े हैं। उन्हें पुनर्जीवित करने की कोशिश करने और पड़ोस से मदद मांगने के बावजूद, उनकी आत्मा ने 2-3 मिनट के भीतर बिना किसी दर्द या पीड़ा के शांतिपूर्वक उनके शरीर को छोड़ दिया। आमतौर पर, अगर दिल की कोई समस्या है, तो लोगों को असुविधा या दर्द महसूस हो

सकता है, लेकिन उन्होंने उस सुबह कुछ भी उल्लेख नहीं किया। मैं पापा के निधन को एक अत्यंत पुण्यात्मा के रूप में देखता हूं जो अपनी इच्छा से शांतिपूर्वक महा-पुण्य-आत्मा के रूप में अपना शरीर छोड़ा हो।

इस दिन मेरे माता-पिता का 60 वर्ष से अधिक का साथ समाप्त हो गया। कुछ साल पहले उन्होंने अपनी शादी की 50वीं सालगिरह मनाई थी। मेरी माँ के लिए आज का दिन बहुत ही दुःख से भरा है जिसका कोई भरपाई नहीं हो सकती.

प्रारंभिक जीवन और शिक्षा

बिहार की राजधानी पटना से लगभग 250 किमी पूर्व में "बुधमा" नामक एक छोटा सा गाँव है। गाँव की जनसंख्या लगभग 1800-2000 (400-500 परिवार, 2023) है। गाँव से निकटतम शहर (सहरसा मधेपुरा) है जो उस समय गांव से कच्ची या टूटी फूटी सड़क से जुड़ा था| निकटतम रेलवे स्टेशन सहरसा (50 किमी) है। 1980 से पहले, गांव में हर साल बाढ़ आती थी और महीनों तक राज्य के बाकी हिस्सों से इसका संपर्क कटा रहता था। गांव में पहला बिजली खंभा 1990 के के दशक में लगा। गांव की क्या स्तिथी रही होगी इसी अंदाज़ा लगाया जा सकता है|

> "1980 के दशक में जब हमलोग बच्चे थे तब सोनपुर से अपने गांव बुधमा जाते समय बस कुछ 5-6 किमी पहले ही उतार देती थी | फिर वह से हमलोग बैल गाड़ी या टमटम (घोड़ा गाड़ी) द्वारा यात्रा करते थे। वस्तुतः हमारा रास्ता खेतों से होकर गुजरता था। मुझे हमेशा यह देखने के लिए सामने की ओर बैठना पसंद था कि मैदान में दौड़ते समय घोड़े की पूँछ कैसे आगे-पीछे हिलती है।

Fig 4. भारत के मानचित्र पर बुधमा गांव मेरी वंशावली की जड़ें इसी गांव में हैं, क्योंकि यह मेरे दादाजी (श्री द्वारिका प्रसाद) और पापा का गृहनगर था। दादा जी का बचपन से लेकर पूरा जीवन वहीं बीता और पालन-पोषण भी उसी गांव में हुआ। एक दिन, मुझे अपने वंश, परदादाओं और पारिवारिक इतिहास के बारे में जानने की जिज्ञासा हुई। पापा ने मुझे एक दिलचस्प कहानी सुनाई.

दादा जी जब बहुत छोटे थे, शायद 7-8 साल के थे, तब वे अपने बड़े भाई और माँ के साथ दूसरे गाँव बुधमा गांव चले आये| मेरे परदादा को काम से संबंधित यात्रा के दौरान कथित तौर पर जहर दिया गया था या मार दिया गया था। मेरे परदादा जाने-माने शिक्षित व्यक्ति थे, जो मुंसी के पद पर कार्यरत थे (मुंसी एक ऐसा पेशा था, जो अमीर लोगों जिसे उन दिनों आम तौर पर जमींदार कहा जाता था के यहां पैसा इकट्ठा करने सहित हिसाब-किताब का काम करते थे| उस गांव में उनके पास कई एकड़ जमीन थी। परिवार संपन्न था. हालाँकि, उनकी मृत्यु के बाद, परिवार की वित्तीय स्थिति खराब हो गई और ब्रिटिश शासन के दौरान देश की स्थिति के कारण कई कठिनाइयों का सामना करना पड़ा। उनके पास जो कुछ भी था मेरी परदादी उसे वहीं छोड़कर गांव से पलायन कर गए और बुधामा गांव में रहने वाले दादा जी की फुआ और फूफा जी के यहां शरण ली।

मेरे दादा जी के फूफा जी बहुत अमीर व्यक्ति थे और उनके पास 100 एकड़ के लगभग कृषि भूमि होगी। बाद में जब मेरे दादाजी बड़े हो गए उन्होंने अपने फूफा जी के लिए काम करना शुरू कर दिया (जैसे कि शुरुआत में उनकी फसलों की देखभाल करना)। उन दिनों शादी भी कम आयु में हो जाती थी तो परिवार की जिम्मेदारियाँ भी आ जाती थी| दादा जी को स्कूल जाने का मौका नहीं मिला तो उन्होंने खुद ही पढाई की - स्व-अध्ययन किया। जिससे वो वह अपने फूफा जी के लिए जमीनों की देखभाल और हिसाब-किताब तथा धन संग्रह का काम करने लगा। इसके बदले में उन्हें साल में प्रति एकड़ खेत के उपज के हिसाब से कुछ किलो चावल या अन्य अनाज मिलता था, यह प्रति माह तय नहीं था कितना मिलेगा। अत: परिवार में वित्तीय एवं आर्थिक स्थिति बहुत अच्छी नहीं थी जीवन चुनौतीपूर्ण बनी रही।

Fig 5. मेरे दादा और (श्री द्वारिका प्रसाद) दादी जी (श्रीमती लीला देवी)

मेरे पापा ने मुझे बताया कि ज्यादातर दिन, वे मुख्य रूप से आलू, मक्के के आटे की रोटी खाते थे, गेहूं के आटे और चावल कभी-कभी एक दावत की तरह होता था। मेरी दादी (श्रीमती लीला देवी) दादा जी को मिलने वाली कुछ किलो चावल बचाती थीं और उन्हें बेचकर कुछ पैसे बचाती थीं और परिवार का भरण-पोषण भी करती थीं । कई वर्षों तक इस तरह से बचत करके, वे उसी गाँव में अपनी कुछ एकड़ कृषि भूमि खरीदने में सक्षम हुए।.

बुधामा में, अधिकांश परिवार गरीबथे, केवल कुछ परिवार जिन्हें जमींदार कहा जाता था, अमीर थे और उनमें से अधिकांश उन अमीर लोगों के लिए काम करते थे। भले ही हमारे पास कुछ ज़मीन थी, बाढ़ प्रभावित कोशी क्षेत्र में स्थित होने के कारण, फसलें अक्सर बाढ़ से नष्ट हो जाती थीं, जिससे खेती से ज्यादा कुछ आर्थिक कमाई नहीं हो पाती थी। हर साल बाढ़ के कारण घर और फसलें नष्ट हो जाती थीं। जो बचता था जिसको बाढ़ के बाद के तबाही से उबरने में निकल जाता था| अपने खेतों में उगी फसलें और सब्जियाँ हमारे परिवार को खिलाने का सहारा था| उस दौर में अनाज ने बदले दूसरे सामान किराने के दुकान से लिया जा सकता था| आज के समय ऐसा सोच भी नहीं सकते| इसलिए बाढ़ से विनाश ने हर साल गांव के गरीब परिवारों को गरीबी से वर्षो निकलने नहीं दिया | उन दिनों दिन में 2 समय का भोजन मिल

जाये यह भी एक चुनैती थी| मेरे दादा जी गाँव में बहुत दयालु और मददगार व्यक्ति थे। गरीबी में भी हरसंभव प्रयास करते थे कि गांव के गरीब परिवारों की मदद की जाये | इसी सोच से उन्होंने जब अपने घर के लिए कुआ बनाये जहा से गांव के लोग पानी बिना रोकटोक के ले सके.

Fig 06. पैतृक गांव के घर में पुराना कुआँ जो अब प्रयोग नहीं हैं

> "हमारे घर की दीवारें और गाँव के अधिकांश घर मिट्टी से खूबसूरती से बनाए गए थे। यह एक गरीब परिवार का प्रतिबिंब हो सकता है, लेकिन यह आश्चर्यजनक था कि पुराने समय में लोग कितने पर्यावरण-हितैषी थे। हम ज्यादातर सर्दियों में अपने गाँव जाते थे, सोने के कमरे में बिस्तर के जगह पर धन का पुआल के मोटी परत बना कर उसपर कम्बल या चादर बिछा कर तैयार किया जाता था। रात में बिस्तर कैसे गर्म रखने के लिए कितनी परते रखनी है ये भी एक कौशल था| दादा जी को हमारे लिए ऐसा बनाने का बहुत शौक था| आमतौर पर ओढ़ने के लिए कम्बल का उपयोग किया जाता था, लेकिन मैं बचपन में सोते समय पुआल के बीच में घुस जाता थे। यहाँ तक की घरो की छते भी पुआल की बानी होती थी"

"हमारे पैतृक घर के पीछे एक पानी का कुआँ था, स्थान ऐसा था कि हमारे घर के आसपास के गरीब परिवारों को पानी के लिए कुएँ तक बिना रोकटोक के पहुंच सके "। कहते है की कुएँ का पानी

बहुत मीठा था । मुझे रस्सी से बंदी बाल्टी की कुएं में डाल कर पानी निकलना बहुत अच्छा लगता था।"

धीरे-धीरे चीजें बदल गईं, बाद में सरकार द्वारा बांध बनाने के कारण बाढ़ जैसी स्थिति कम हो गई और किसान कुछ फसलें उगाने में सक्षम हो गए जिनका वे उपयोग भी कर सकते हैं और बेच भी सकते थे । उगाई जाने वाली प्राथमिक फसल धान थी। उन दिनों धन के फसल से चावल बनाने की पूरी प्रक्रिया गांव के लोग आपने घर पर ही करते थे मेरी दादी धान को संसाधित करके चावल बनाती थीं और फिर वह चावल से चूरा बनाती थीं। चावल को पूरे वर्ष के लिए संग्रहित करने का भी एक अलग ही तरीका था| मिट्टी से बने कंटेनर (जिसे कोठी कहा जाता था) में संग्रहित करती थीं, जो मिट्टी से बना एक बड़ा बेलनाकार का लगभग २०० लीटर छमता का होता था - अनाज भरने के लिए ऊपर से खुलता था और निकालने के लिए एक नीचे छोटा सा छेड़ होता था| हमारे घर में ऐसे कम से कम 5 होंगे

जब हमारे खेत में चावल उगाए जाने लगे, तो हमारी स्थिति थोड़ी बेहतर हुई और दैनिक भोजन थोड़ा और बेहतर हुआ जैसे की नाश्ता और दोपहर का भोजन मुख्य रूप से दही और चूरा होने लगा, इसलिए यह पापा का अपने पूरे जीवन में पसंदीदा भोजन बना (दही और चूरा)।

> "मेरी दादी एक अत्यधिक कुशल महिला थीं, जो असाधारण रूप से मीठा और मलाईदार दही बनाने के लिए प्रसिद्ध थीं। चूँकि हमारे पास एक गाय थी, इसलिए वह आमतौर पर इसे हमारी ही गाय के दूध से तैयार करती थी। वह दूध को मिट्टी के बर्तन में लकड़ी की आग पर तब तक गर्म करती थी जब तक कि उसकी मात्रा आधी न हो जाए। बाद में, वह इसे दूसरे मिट्टी के बर्तन में रख देती थी और रात भर घर की छत से लटका देती थी।"

पापा का जन्म भारत की आज़ादी से कुछ साल पहले 1943 में उसी गाँव में हुआ था। पापा कुल मिलाकर पाँच भाई-बहन थे। पापा परिवार में सबसे बड़े बेटे थे और मेरी बड़ी फुआ के बाद दूसरे सबसे बड़े बच्चे थे। पापा का जन्म मेरी बड़ी फुआ के बाद हुआ था, हालाँकि,

उनके बीच 2 अन्य बहनें पैदा हुईं और अप्रत्याशित रूप से मर गईं। मेडिकल सुभिधाये उस समय ना के बारबार थी मेरे दो चाचा का नाम है श्री मोदन मोहन प्रसाद और श्री रामचंद्र प्रसाद, हमलोग गावो में अपने चाचा को छोटे पापा से ही सम्बोदित करते थे/है

Fig 7. पैतृक गांव का घर बुधमा

1950 और 1960 के दशक के दौरान शिक्षा प्राप्त करना कोई आसान काम नहीं था, इसके लिए बहुत प्रयास, समय, दृढ़ता और समर्पण की आवश्यकता पड़ती थी। 1951 में बिहार में समग्र साक्षरता दर 13.49% थी | दादा जी एक दूरदर्शी व्यक्ति थे| जिन्होंने शिक्षा को किसी के जीवन का सबसे महत्वपूर्ण हिस्सा माना। उनका ये दृष्टिकोण इस बात से पता चलता है की उनके सभी छह बच्चों - तीन बेटों और तीन बेटियों - ने उस समय माध्यमिक शिक्षा प्राप्त की। दादाजी ने यह सुनिश्चित किया कि पापा को उचित शिक्षा मिले क्योंकि उन दिनों गाँव में प्राथमिक और माध्यमिक विद्यालय नहीं था|

मेरे पापा मेरी बड़ी फुआ के बहुत ही लाडले थे। फुआ उनसे इतना प्यार करती थी कि शादी दूसरे गांव में होने के बाद भी फु आ और बड़े फूफा जी ने पापा को 4-5 वर्ष की आयु में अपने घर ले गए। पापा ने अपनी शुरुआती पढ़ाई अपनी सबसे बड़ी बहन के यहाँ रहकर की। यह उस समय भाई-बहन के बीच बंधन, रिश्तो और प्यार का स्तर कुछ अलग ही होता था जो धीरे धीरे लुप्त होता जा रहा है । कुछ वर्षों के बाद, पापा गाँव वापस आ गए

क्योंकि मेरी दादी जी को भी उनकी याद आती थी। चूँकि, उनके गाँव में कोई स्कूल नहीं था, इसलिए पापा दूसरे गाँव में प्राथमिक और माध्यमिक विद्यालयों में पढ़ने के लिए हर दिन 2-3 किमी पैदल चल कर जाते थे | इस प्रकार पापा ने अपनी प्राथमिक शिक्षा पूरी की। दादा जी को आमतौर पर ग्रामीणों या शिक्षको से पापा से सम्बंधित कोई शिकायत नहीं मिली । पापा स्वभाव से एक सरल और ईमानदार छात्र थे।

पापा को अपनी शिक्षा प्राप्त करने के लिए जबरदस्त चुनौतियों मुश्किलों का सामना करना पड़ा। उनके पास हार मानकर खेती करने का विकल्प था, लेकिन कठिनाइयों के बावजूद, उन्होंने पढ़ाई करने और अपनी शिक्षा पूरी करने के लिए हर संभव प्रयास किया। पढ़ाई के साथ-साथ पापा ने कुछ पैसे कमाने और दादा जी का सहयोग करने के लिए छोटे बच्चों को टूशन पढ़ाना शुरू कर दिया। दादा जी की आर्थिक स्थिति अभी भी अच्छी नहीं थी, क्योंकि वे 6 बच्चों के परिवार का भरण-पोषण कर रहे थे और कृषि उपज भी पर्याप्त नहीं थी। पापा न केवल अपना भरण-पोषण कर रहे थे बल्कि दादा जी को बचत भी कर के दे रहे थे।

बेहतर शिक्षा पाने के लिए अपने तमाम संघर्ष के बाद, उन्होंने 1959 में मिडिल स्कूल बोर्ड परीक्षा उत्तीर्ण की। चूँकि आगे की पढ़ाई के लिए आस-पास कोई स्कूल नहीं था, इसलिए वह मधेपुरा में एमपीएचएस (उस समय बहुद्देशीय माध्यमिक विद्यालय कहा जाता था) से इंटरमीडिएट करने के लिए अपनी बहन के घर वापस चले गए। हमारी जानकारी के अनुसार पूरे क्षेत्र में केवल 2 छात्र ही उत्तीर्ण हुए थे।

उन दिनों हमारे समाज में कम उम्र में शादी कर देना बहुत आम बात थी। जबकि पापा ने ग्रेजुएशन (बीए की डिग्री) करने एक दूसरे शहर बेगूसराय चले गए क्योंकि वहां पर ही उन दिने कॉलेज के पढाई होती थी| बेगुसराय में पढ़ाई के दौरान ही उनकी शादी हो गयी । मेरे नाना बेगुसराय के बाघी नामक गाँव से रहते थे| वे शिक्षित थे और सोनपुर में रेलवे मंडल कार्यालय में टाइपिस्ट के रूप में कार्यरत थे और पूरे परिवार के साथ सोनपुर में एक मकान में किराए के में रहते थे।

शादी के वक्त पापा सिर्फ 19 साल के थे और मां 16 साल की थीं| अम्मा ने अपनी 10वीं की बोर्ड परीक्षा पहले ही पूरी कर ली थी और प्रथम श्रेणी से उत्तीर्ण हुई थी। उन्हें गांव के एक स्कूल में अध्यापिका की नौकरी मिल गई, जिसका बाद में सरकारीकरण हो गया । स्कूल में उनके सहित केवल 2 महिला शिक्षक थीं। सोनपुर पापा के लिए कर्मभूमि कैसे बनी, इसमें अम्मा बहुत महत्वपूर्ण कड़ी हैं।

पापा ने बीए की डिग्री पूरी करने के लिए अपनी पढ़ाई जारी रखी, हालांकि शादी के बाद जिम्मेदारियां बढ़ गईं। अम्मा बहुत अच्छी, तेज और गंभीर छात्रा थीं। उन्होंने शादी पहले ही एक शिक्षिका के रूप में काम करना शुरू कर दिया था लेकिन वह आगे पढ़ना भी चाहती थीं। अम्मा मेरे नाना के 10 भाई-बहनों - 7 बहनों और 3 भाइयों - में सबसे बड़ी संतान थीं।

नाना तरफ की आर्थिक स्थिति भी अच्छी नहीं थी। अम्मा को याद है कि ऐसे भी दिन थे जब वे दिन में केवल एक बार खाना खाते थे, दो बार खाना बहुत कम ही नसीब होता था, होता भी था तो सिर्फ चावल, दाल और चोखा तक ही सीमित रहते थे। दोनों ने इतनी काम उम्र ही दोनों तरफ के परिवारों के पढ़ाई और पारिवारिक जिम्मेदारियां उठा ली. दोनों ने व्यक्तिगत रूप से अपने प्रत्येक भाई-बहन को पढ़ाने और गाँव में बच्चों को ट्यूशन देने जैसे अतिरिक्त काम करके परिवारों को आर्थिक रूप से समर्थन देने की भूमिका निभाई।

> "परिवार के वरिष्ठ सदस्य के नाते मेरे ही नहीं परिवार के सभी सदस्यों के संरक्षक, अभिभावक, मार्गदर्शक थे | उनके तथा बड़ी दीदी के मार्गदर्शन में हम सभी नवो भाई और बहनों (६बहने+३भाईयों) का पढ़ाई लिखाई हुआ । तथा इनके दिशानिर्देश से तीन बहनें मुन्ना दीदी, गुड़ी दीदी और आशा दीदी सरकारी शिक्षिका सेवा में प्रतिनिधित्व की।" श्री अजित कुमार सिन्हा (बड़े मामा)

बीए की पढ़ाई पूरी करने के बाद पापा ने शिक्षक की नौकरी के लिए कई जगह कोशिश की। जिस स्कूल में अम्मा अध्यापिका थीं, उसी स्कूल में उन्हें अस्थायी अध्यापक का पद मिल गया। बाद में,

1965 में पापा का चयन सोनपुर के उसी स्कूल में प्रधानाध्यापक पद के लिए हो गया, क्योंकि प्रधानाध्यापक पद के लिए बीए की डिग्री होना आवश्यक था। 1960 के दशक में बीए डिग्री धारक या स्नातक होना बहुत आम बात नहीं थी।

Keshav Prasad Ambasta

Madan Mohan Prasad

Ramchandra Prasad

Fig 09. पापा अपने दो भाइयों के साथ (श्री मदन मोहन प्रसाद और श्री रामचंद्र प्रसाद)

मेरे माता-पिता की स्मृति के अनुसार, पापा का वेतन रु. 60 और अम्मा का रु. 40, लेकिन शिक्षक के रूप में अपनी नौकरी के पहले कुछ वर्षों के दौरान इतने बड़े परिवार का भरण-पोषण करने के लिए पर्याप्त नहीं थे।

गांव की सच्ची हास्यास्पद घटना पापा के मुख से

"शादियों में परम्परा है कि सिन्दूर दान के पश्चात तथा दोपहर के भोजन से पूर्व नवविवाहित वधू को घुंघट (घोंघटा) दिया जाता है। वर पक्ष की ओर से वधू को गहने और कपड़े दिए जाते हैं,कमोवेश अभी भी यह प्रथा प्रचलन में है। परन्तु पांच दशक पूर्व इस प्रथा से पहले दोनों पक्षों की इम्तिहान और बहुत ही दिलचस्प वाद-विवाद प्रतियोगिता भी होता था । इस बहस के लिए शिक्षित व्यक्तियों की आवश्यकता थी, और मेरे पिता, सुशिक्षित होने के कारण, हमेशा शादियों के दौरान इन चर्चाओं में भाग लेते थे।

मेरे पिता जी एक दिलचस्प घटना का बड़े प्रेम से वर्णन किया करते थे। वधू पक्ष के दरवाजा पर लोगों से भरे खचाखच इस प्रतियोगिता को देखने के लिए भीड़ लगी हुई थी। मेरे पिता जी वधू पक्ष की ओर से प्रतिनिधित्व करने कुर्सी पर बैठे हुए थे।इसी बीच गाँव के एक प्रतिष्ठित व्यक्ति ने ऊंचे स्वर में बोले फला का बेटा को जल्दी से बुलाने को कहा, जो पटना शहर में पढ़ रहे थे और

ग्रीष्म अवकाश में गांव आए थे, वधू पक्ष की ओर से भाग लेने के लिए बुलाया गया। वाद-विवाद प्रतियोगिता शुरू हो गई, शुरू में हिन्दी में सवाल जबाव चलता रहा,इसी बीच वर पक्ष की ओर से अपना दबदबा बनाए रखने के लिए अंग्रेजी में प्रश्न किया,सभा में सन्नाटा छा गया क्योंकि बात बहुत कम ब्यक्ति को समझ में आया,पिता जी जबाब देने के लिए खड़े हुए तभी पिता जी के साथी बोले,केशव जी आप नहीं इस अग्रेज का जबाब मेरा बच्चा (जो पटना में पढ़ाई कर रहा था) देगा। फिर क्या था, लड़के ने

माइक्रोफोन उठाया और, "Flood (बाढ़)" पर अंग्रेजी में निबंध वह धारा प्रवाह 3-4 मि.बोलता गया। अंग्रेजी में इस भावुक भाषण सुनकर सभी आश्चर्यचकित थे दो मिनट तक पिन-ड्रॉप साइलेंस छा गया हालाँकि वधू और वर पक्ष इस्तेमाल की गई जटिल अंग्रेजी भाषा को समझ नहीं सका, लेकिन यह सभी के लिए स्पष्ट था कि उत्तर उन्नत था, और पूछा गया प्रश्न चुनौतीपूर्ण था। वर पक्ष कुछ बोलते नतीजा घोषित हो गया जीत गए जीत गए........... सभी ग्रामीण उछल पड़े ।हम खेल में विजयी हुए और पूरी महफिल में तालियां गूंज उठीं। सही में कोई नहीं जान पाया कि क्या सवाल और क्या जबाब था चारों ओर वाह वाह होने लगा तथा सभा समाप्त की घोषणा कर दी गई।"

उनके व्यक्तित्व के बारे में

पापा बहुत ही साधारण जीवन जीना पसंद करते थे, वे उच्च नैतिक मूल्यों वाले एक "जमीन से जुड़े" या "विनम्र" व्यक्ति थे - शांत और मिलनसार व्यक्ति थे। कठिन परिस्थितियों में भी वे शांत रहना और क्रोध नहीं करना उनकी विशेषता थी | वह लड़ाई से नहीं, बल्कि बात करके और एक-दूसरे को समझकर समस्याओं का समाधान करने में विश्वास करते थे।

"जब मैं दिल्ली में 10वीं कक्षा में पढ़ता था तो पापा ने मुझसे कहा करते थे कि अपने दोस्तों से यह दिखावा या झूठ मत बोलना कि तुम्हारे पापा-मम्मी प्रिंसिपल हैं और हम बिहार में एक अमीर परिवार हैं। दरअसल, उन्होंने मेरे व्यवहार और गतिविधियों से सही संकेत मिल रहा था की

शायद मैं बड़ा बनाने का दिखवा तो नहीं कर रहा हूँ। वह दिखावे में विश्वास नहीं करते थे".

उनका हृदय कोमल एवं दयालु था। उनके मन में किसी के प्रति द्वेष नहीं था. चीजों से निपटने का उनका तरीका इस बात का एक अच्छा उदाहरण है कि कैसे मित्रवत रहकर एक खुशहाल जीवन जिया जाए और गुस्से या तर्क-वितर्क से चीजों को खराब न होने दिया जाए। ऐसी दुनिया में जहां लोग कभी-कभी आपस में नहीं मिलते, पापा का शांतिपूर्ण और मैत्रीपूर्ण रहने का तरीका एक अच्छा जीवन जीने का एक शानदार तरीका है।

पापा को जानने वाले या उनके साथ काम करने वाले सैकड़ों लोगों से बातचीत के दौरान मैंने कभी उनके बारे में एक भी नकारात्मक बात नहीं सुनी। कई लोगों का एक बहुत ही आश्चर्यजनक कथन था "वह मुझसे/हमसे या हमारे परिवार से सबसे अधिक प्यार करते थे "। इसका मतलब है कि उन्होंने हर किसी को महत्वपूर्ण और प्यार का एहसास कराया, जो कि एक व्यक्ति का एक बहुत ही अनोखा गुण है।

"सर जी को बहुत कम गुस्सा आता था, लेकिन जब भी गुस्सा आता था तो सिर्फ मुस्कुराहट और हंसी ही आती थी, वो एक शब्द जरूर कहते थे, "भुसगोल, काम धंधा कुछ नहीं फूटानी लंबा चौरा काम चोर", ये शब्द मुझे आज भी याद हैं। लेकिन उनके गुस्से पर भी हम मुस्कुराते थे और हंसते थे।" -राकेश राज सिंह

"वह घर, परिवार से लेकर समाज, शहर के बच्चों और लड़कियों तक सभी को प्रेरित करते थे। उन्होंने सदैव युवतियों और युवाओं को शिक्षा के लिए प्रोत्साहित किया और अपने जीवन के अंतिम क्षण तक शिक्षा दान करते रहे" - श्री हेम वर्मा

23 साल की उम्र में पापा कन्या मध्य विद्यालय पहाड़ीचक सोनपुर में प्रधानाध्यापक के पद पर कार्यरत हो गये. शिक्षण के प्रति उनके समर्पण और ईमानदारी ने उन्हें जल्द ही गाँव और आस-पास के स्कूलों में पहचान मिल गयी| उनके पढ़ाने का विषय हिंदी, अंग्रेजी, संस्कृत था। इसके अलावा, परिवार को आगे बढ़ाने

के लिए वह गांवों में बच्चों को ट्यूशन देने का भी काम कर रहे थे।

"आज, मैं एक कंपनी में निदेशक हूं, बड़े पापा की वजह से मैं अपनी कंपनी के मालिक के लिए सबसे भरोसेमंद व्यक्ति हूं। उनका ईमानदारी और सत्यनिष्ठा से जीवन जीना मुझे बचपन से ही प्रेरित करता रहा और मैंने उन चरित्रों को अपने अंदर आत्मसात कर लिया। उनकी प्रेरणा और मुझे दिल्ली में एक छोटी सी नौकरी दिलाने में मदद ने मेरे करियर और भविष्य को उज्जवल किया ।" मनिंदर कुमार सिन्हा (संजय भैया), जयपुर

एक घटना जो मुझे अच्छी तरह याद है, एक बार पापा मुझे एक महिला की झोपड़ी में ले गये जो बुधामा में हमारे पड़ोस में थी। वह एक बूढ़ी गरीब महिला थी जो बांस की डंडियों से बनी एक छोटी सी झोपड़ी में अकेली रहती थी। वह फर्श पर मिट्टी से बने एक छोटे से खाना पकाने के स्थान पर बैठी थी, उस झोपड़ी में लगभग कुछ भी नहीं था। मेरे पापा और दादा जी समय-समय पर उसकी मदद करते थे। पापा ने मुझसे उनके पैर छूने और आशीर्वाद लेने को कहा। मैं करीब 12 साल का युवा था और ऐसा करने में थोड़ा झिझक रहा था, लेकिन मैंने उनके कहे अनुसार ही किया। बाद में मैंने पूछा कि वह इतनी महत्वपूर्ण क्यों थी कि आप मुझे उसके पास ले गये। इस घटना का मेरे जीवन में बड़ा असर हुआ जो उन्होंने मुझे उस दिन सिखाया था। तो उन्होंने कहा कि हमें गरीब लोगों का सम्मान करना चाहिए और उनकी मदद करनी चाहिए, उनका आशीर्वाद बहुत शक्तिशाली होता है. उन्होंने एक पुरानी घटना को भी याद किया कि स्कूल और कॉलेज के दिनों में उनके पास घड़ी नहीं थी, वह मेरे दादा जी से कह रहे थे कि वह एक घड़ी खरीद सकते हैं क्योंकि कभी-कभी समय पर पहुंचना मुश्किल होता है और लोगों से घड़ी के लिए समय पूछना पड़ता है। जैसे कि निजी ट्यूशन देना और कॉलेज में पढ़ने के लिए समय पर जाना,

लेकिन, उस दौर में हमारा परिवार घड़ी खरीदने की स्थिति में नहीं था। उस समय जब बातचीत चल रहा ही तो वह बूढ़ी महिला हमारे घर में बैठी थी और उसने कहा था कि "एक दिन तुम इतने सक्षम हो जाओगे कि एक नहीं बल्कि कई घड़ियाँ खरीद सकोगे।" दरअसल, कई साल बाद उनकी बातें सच साबित हुईं।

गाँव में और उनके शिक्षक मित्रों के बीच, कई लोग शादी की बातचीत के लिए उन्हें अपने साथ ले जाते थे, खासकर जब बात उनकी बेटियों की हो (आगुआ करना कहते है)। वह दूल्हे के परिवार के साथ बातचीत करने में वास्तव में बहुत अच्छे थे । गाँवों में या रिश्तेदारों की शादियों में, वह एक अभिभावक की तरह काम करते थे, दूल्हा और दुल्हन के परिवारों के बीच समस्याओं को सुलझाने के लिए हमेशा तैयार रहते थे, चाहे वह किसी भी पक्ष में हों। उनका एक कथन बहुत बार सुना की शादी विवाह में थोड़ा बहुत होता रहता है जाने दीजिये| बातचीत करने में उसके इतने अच्छे होने का एक कारण यह था कि वह एक उत्कृष्ट श्रोता था। बोलने से पहले वह दूसरों की बातें ध्यान से सुनते थे | वह कभी भी अप्रासंगिक बातों से परेशान नहीं होते थे, इसलिए स्थिति के बारे में सोचकर शांति से जवाब देते थे। इसीलिए उनके उत्तर समझ में आते थे और लोगों को आश्वस्त करते थे।

> "उनकी पहचान केवल शिक्षा के क्षेत्र में नहीं थी। बल्कि उन्होंने सामाजिक, वैवाहिक और सामाजिक सुधार कार्यक्रमों में भी बढ़-चढ़कर हिस्सा लिया। उन्होंने अनगिनत परिवारों और समाजों के विवाह योग्य लड़कों और लड़कियों के विकास में योगदान दिया। श्री अजीत कुमार सिन्हा (बड़े मामा)

छोटे बच्चों के साथ उनका हास्यबोध अद्भुत था। मेरे बेटे यश ने मुझे बताया कि उसने दादा जी से सीखा है कि लूडो या कोई भी खेल कैसे हास्य के साथ और मजाकिया तरीके से खेला जाता है, जीत या हार को ज्यादा गंभीरता से नहीं लिया जाता।

मेरी दीदी एक बार पटना में एक परीक्षा के लिए गयी थी साथ में पापा और उनका छोटा बेटा जानू (शांतनु उर्फ जानू) जो उस समय 5-6 वर्ष का होगा। जब दीदी परीक्षा देने चली गयी

तो जानू रोने लगा | उनका ध्यान कही और भटकाने के लिए पापा उसको पूरा पटना के मुख्या जगह दिखने ले गए|

यह संयोग ही था कि पापा की शादी सबको शिक्षा को लेकर एक जैसी सोच रखने वाले परिवार में हुई। चूँकि मेरे माता-पिता दोनों शिक्षक थे - अम्मा 10 भाई-बहनों में सबसे बड़ी थीं और पापा चार छोटे भाई-बहनों में सबसे बड़े बेटे थे - उन्होंने संयुक्त रूप से परिवार के दोनों पक्षों के लिए शिक्षा को सर्वोच्च प्राथमिकता बनाने का निर्णय लिया। उनकी प्रतिबद्धता के परिणामस्वरूप, उन सभी ने कम से कम कॉलेज स्तर की शिक्षा (उन दिनों इंटरमीडिएट) हासिल की, और कई, विशेष रूप से हमारे परिवार की महिलाएं, बिहार के सरकारी स्कूलों में शिक्षक नियुक हुई ।

शिक्षा निश्चित रूप से परिवार में समृद्धि और प्रगति लाती है। पिछले कुछ वर्षों में हमारी वित्तीय स्थिति में सुधार हुआ है। प्रगतिशील सोच के परिणामस्वरूप वर्षों में जीवन की गुणवत्ता में सुधार हुआ और अगली पीढ़ी को उच्च लक्ष्यों के लिए प्रेरणा मिली।

एक आदर्श शिक्षक के रूप में - सोनपुर एक कर्मभूमि

सोनपुर: सोनपुर अतीत में दो चीजों के लिए प्रसिद्ध रहा है: i) एक प्रसिद्ध पशु मेला (जो दुनिया का सबसे बड़ा पशु मेला माना जाता है) जहाँ हाथी, ऊंट और घोड़ों से लेकर पक्षियों तक सभी जानवर बेचने के लिए उपलब्ध थे और ii) अब तक का सबसे लंबा रेलवे प्लेटफॉर्म - 1990 तक शायद| यह बिहार के छपरा (सारण) जिले में 2 पवित्र नदियों गंगा और गंडक संगम पर स्थित है| पटना हवाई अड्डे से 25 किमी दूर स्थित है। सोनपुर की एक और बहुत महत्वपूर्ण पहचान हिंदू मंदिर "हरि-हर" है, एक दुर्लभ मंदिर जहां शिव और विष्णु दोनों गर्वगृह में रहते हैं और पूजा की जाती है। इस मंदिर के कारण इसे हरिहरश्रेत्र भी कहा जाता है।

Fig 10. पापा अपने स्कूल के शिक्षक साथियों के साथ

पापा की शिक्षा पूरी होने के बाद सोनपुर उनकी कर्मभूमि बन गयी। अम्मा (श्रीमती रुक्मिणी कुमारी) के जिक्र के बिना पापा की जिंदगी और उनका कर्मभूमि की कहानी अधूरी है। अम्मा भी उन कुछ लड़कियों में से एक थीं जिन्होंने 1962 में 10वीं कक्षा उत्तीर्ण की और उसी स्कूल में 1962 में शिक्षिका के रूप में नियुक हुई| मेरे नाना जी (श्री हरिशंकर प्रसाद) समान रूप से दूरदर्शी थे, उन्होंने लड़का लड़की में भेदभाव किये बिना अपने सभी बच्चों के लिए शिक्षा सुनिश्चित की। अम्मा, अपने 10 भाई-बहनों में सबसे बड़ी होने के कारण, अपनी पढ़ाई के प्रति असाधारण रूप से समर्पित थीं। वह उस समय इस शैक्षिक स्तर तक पहुंचने वाली जिले की कुछ लड़कियों में से एक थीं, जब 1951 में बिहार में लड़कियों की साक्षरता दर केवल 5% थी।

Fig 10a. मेरे नाना जी और नानी जी

अम्मा का पापा के जीवन में बहुत बड़ा योगदान रहा है उनके सहयोग और सहमति के बिना पापा का पूरी तरह से शिक्षा और समाज को जो उन्होंने अपना वक्त दिया वो संभव नहीं हो पता| अम्मा लगातार पापा के कार्यो में मदद करती रहती थी| उनके सहमति का इससे बड़ा उदाहरण क्या हो सकता है कि मेरी बड़ी मौसी (श्रीमती रीता सिन्हा - मुन्ना मौसी) जिनका शादी के कुछ समय में ही मौसा जी का निधन हो गया, उनको अपने यहाँ रख कर पढाई कराया और शिक्षक प्रशिक्षण स्कूल से दाखिला कराया जिससे उनको सरकारी स्कूल में शिक्षक की नौकरी मिल गयी आत्मनिर्भर बानी| उन दिनों पति के मृत्यु के बाद महिलाओ को समाज में बहुत ही तकलीफों का सामना करना परता था| दूसरी शादी की समाज में इज्जाजत नहीं थी और उनको अपने घरवालों के दया पर जीना पड़ता था| मौसी मेरी लिए माँ के सामान ही थी उनसे मुझे बहुत प्यार दिया और ललन पोषण किया एक माँ की तरह

मेरी अम्मा की हैंडराइटिंग (हस्तलिपि) बहुत ही सुन्दर बिलकुल मोतीओ जैसी थी| मैंने अक्सर अम्मा से लेखनी सम्बंदित कार्य करते देखा है जो पापा उनको करने के लिए देते थे| अम्मा भी शिक्षण की गुणवत्ता के प्रति बहुत गंभीर थी| अपने स्कूल में वो सभी कक्षा बहुत तैयारी से करती थी| घर में हम सभी भाई

बहनो को रोजना अम्मा ही पड़ती थी| मुझे तो खासकर के पिटाई भी परती थी क्योंकि मैं बहनो जैसा पड़ने पर ध्यान नहीं देता था| अम्मा का शिक्षादान के प्रति निष्ठा का उदाहरण है कि आज भी उनके ७७ वर्ष के उम्र में रोजना गांव के ३-४ बच्चे ५-१० क्लास के बच्चे पढ़ने आते है उन्होंने पापा के मुर्त्यु के बाद भी ये जारी रखा और उन बच्चो के प्रति वो चिंतिति भी रहती है की ठीक से नहीं पड़ेंगे तो क्या होगा उनका | अक्सर उनको मैंने बच्चो को समझाते और प्यार से डाटते देखता हूँ

उनका जीवन शिक्षा की परिवर्तनकारी, अपने छात्रों के प्रति दृढ़ प्रतिबद्धता और करुणा, ईमानदारी, अखंडता और समर्पण के सिद्धांतों पर बनी विरासत का एक प्रमाण है। दरअसल उनकी नियुक्ति 1965 में प्रधानाध्यापक के रूप में की गई थी, यानी उन पर स्कूल चलाने और पढ़ाने दोनों की जिम्मेदारी थी। उन्हें समय पर स्कूल पहुंचना और सभी शिक्षण अवधियों को पूरा करना और अंत में समय पर निकलना पसंद था। पापा ने शिक्षण की गुणवत्ता का बहुत ध्यान रखते थे कि शिक्षण निर्धारित समय सारिणी के साथ किया जाए, यह अधिकांश स्कूलों में सामान्य बात नहीं थी। अपने पुरे प्रधानाध्यापक कार्यकाल में वे 3 स्कूलों में रहे| जिस स्कूल में वे गए वो स्कूल के अनुशासन, अच्छी शिक्षा के लिए जनजाती थी| उनका स्कूल सबसे अधिक छात्रों की संख्या और उपस्थिति के लिए प्रसिद्ध था।

Fig 11. अम्मा के साथ मुन्ना मौसी

उनके स्कूल में जब शिक्षक और छात्र उन्हें स्कूल के गेट में प्रवेश करते देखते थे, तो सभी जल्दी से तितर-बितर हो कक्षा में प्रवेश कर कर जाते थे । पापा एक सख्त शिक्षक नहीं थे, लेकिन वह एक आदर्श थे और इस बात पर जोर देते थे कि साथी शिक्षक नियमों का पालन करें, तभी हम छात्रों को सही ढंग से पढ़ा सकते है उनका आदर्श बन सकते है|

> "एक बार उन्होंने एक शिक्षक से 7वीं कक्षा के छात्रों को अंग्रेजी पढ़ाने के लिए कहा। वह अध्यापक अंग्रेजी पढ़ाने में बहुत सक्षम नहीं थे । जब पापा के पास अपनी स्वयं की शिक्षण कक्षा नहीं होती थी तो वे आमतौर पर शिक्षण गुणवत्ता का आकलन करने और कक्षा में भ्रमण करते थे न की ऑफिस में बैठे रहना । जब यह टीचर क्लास ले रही थी तो पापा को एहसास हुआ कि वह अंग्रेजी गलत सलत पढा रही है । इसलिए, बाद में उन्होंने उससे पूछा तो शिक्षक ने बताया की उनको अंग्रेजी अच्छे से नहीं आती है उसके बाद एक अन्य सक्षम शिक्षक को अंग्रेजी के लिए नियुक्त किया वे इस बात का ध्यान रखते थे की शिक्षक सक्षम हो पढ़ाने में।"

मेरे पापा छात्रों के सर्वांगीण विकास में विश्वास करते थे, इसलिए वह केवल पढ़ाई तक ही सीमित नहीं थे, बल्कि उन्होंने पाठ्येतर गतिविधियों, खेल गतिविधियों, कार्यक्रमों और समारोहों को भी सुनिश्चित किया करते थे । उनके विद्यालय ने (खरिका) कई वर्षों तक सर्वोत्तम सरस्वती पूजा का आयोजन किया था|

समर्पण और नवीन शिक्षण शैली एक आदर्श शिक्षक की पहचान है। उनकी शैली उन दिनों में नई शैली ही कही जाएगी| उन दिनों गुरु-शिष्य परंपरा समाज के लिए प्रमुख और सामान्य थी। आमतौर पर, माता-पिता छात्र के बेहतर भविष्य को ध्यान में रखते हुए अपने बच्चों को पढ़ाई के मामले में शिक्षकों को सौंप देते हैं। शिक्षकों के लिए सख्त होना और सज़ा देना आम बात थी और छात्र अक्सर उनसे डरते थे। लेकिन मेरे पापा अलग थे| ऐसे समय में जब शिक्षकों को बहुत गंभीर माना जाता था, उन्होंने कोशिश की कक्षा और छात्र सहज बने| वह चाहते थे कि छात्र बिना डरे

प्रश्न पूछने में सहज महसूस करें। अन्य शिक्षकों के विपरीत, वह कभी छात्रों पर क्रोध नहीं करते थे और न ही उन्हें दंडित करते थे। इसके बजाय, वे बच्चो का विश्वास जितने की कोशिश करते थे ताकि बच्चे उनपर भरोसा कर अपने मन की बात खुल कर कर सके. उन्होंने वर्षों तक भरोसा और भरोसा कायम किया। पढाई में दिलचस्प उदाहरणों का उपयोग करके सीखना आसान बना देते थे| वह जानते थे कि कमजोर छात्र कौन हैं और उन्हें कैसे संभालना है।

> "कई लोग सरकारी स्कूल शिक्षक के रूप में 6 घंटे की ड्यूटी करने के बाद अपने परिवार तक ही सीमित रहते हैं। लेकिन हमारे मौसा जी बिल्कुल भी ऐसे नहीं थे. सरकारी सेवा में रहते हुए वे सामाजिक कार्यों में, जन कल्याण में या शैक्षिक गतिविधियों और आधिकारिक कार्यों में समय व्यतीत करते थे" अश्वनी कुमार (मोनू)

> "केशव सर हमारे क्षेत्र सोनपुर के बहुत प्रसिद्ध शिक्षक थे। वे हमारे गाँव के साथ-साथ पूरे सोनपुर के हर घर के पसंदीदा शिक्षक थे, इसीलिए हर माता-पिता की दिली इच्छा होती थी कि केशव सर उनके बच्चे को पढ़ाएँ, जो उनके उज्ज्वल भविष्य को बनाने में सहायक साबित होंगे। जब हम गलतियाँ करते थे तो वह हमें प्यार से समझाते थे। वह समय-समय पर हमें आगे बढ़ने के लिए मार्गदर्शन करते रहते थे।" राकेश राज सिंह (पूर्व छात्र)

जब मैं 1991 से 1993 तक दिल्ली में स्कूल में था, तब मुझे लगातार हिंदी और अंग्रेजी विषयों में सर्वोच्च अंक प्राप्त होते थे। मेरे शिक्षक इन भाषाओं में मेरे लेखन की गुणवत्ता से आश्चर्यचकित थे। उन्हें तब तक आश्चर्य हुआ जब तक उन्हें पता नहीं चला कि मैं शिक्षकों के परिवार से आता हूं। सोनपुर में घर पर मेरी गर्मी की छुट्टियों के दो महीनों के दौरान, पापा मुझे आगामी वर्ष के लिए अंग्रेजी और हिंदी का पूरा पाठ्यक्रम पढ़ाते थे। उनका शिक्षण मेरे अंग्रेजी ज्ञान का मूल है जिसने मुझे उच्च अध्ययन और अंग्रेजी बोलने वाले विदेशी देशों (ऑस्ट्रेलिया, यूएसए, यूके) में मदद की।

60 वर्ष की आयु में सेवानिवृत्ति का मतलब उनकी सेवा का अंत नहीं था; इसके बजाय, इसने एक नए अध्याय की शुरुआत को चिह्नित किया। अगले दो दशकों तक, उन्होंने लगातार पीढ़ियों के जीवन पर अमिट छाप छोड़ते हुए पढ़ाना, मार्गदर्शन करना, मार्गदर्शन करना और समर्थन देना जारी रखा। गाँव के गर्ल्स हाई स्कूलों सहित कई स्कूलों के प्रधानाध्यापक, शिक्षक, छात्र और प्रिंसिपल पिछले 2 दशकों में उनके योगदान के प्रमाण हैं।

आजकल मैं देखता हूँ की माँ बाप कितने आपने बच्चो पर पढ़ाई और करियर चुनाव पर दबाव बनाते है| कितने मनोविज्ञानिक का मानना है की बच्चो को जिस विषय से लगाव हो उनको उसी क्षेत्र जाने दिया जाये जिससे की वो अपने जॉब को काम को आनंद पूर्वक पुरे मन से कर सके | मैं कभी कभी बहुत आश्चर्य होता हूँ की मेरे पापा कितने आधुनिक विचार के थे कि उन्होंने मुझे विषय और अपने करियर को लेकर पूरी आजादी दी कि मुझे क्या पड़ना है कहा पड़ना है और किस श्रेत्र में जाना है. उनके इसी आजादी कारण ही मैं देश और विदेश में शीर्ष संस्थान से पढ़ाई करके आज विदेश में पिछले १५ वर्षो से यूरोप के प्रतिष्ठित कंपनियाँ में वैज्ञानिक के पद में से कार्यरत हूँ और आपने काम को आनदंपुर्वक कर रहा हूँडॉक्टर बनाना चाहता था | एकलौता लड़का होने के बावजूद भी पापा और अम्मा ने मुझे अपने से दूर दिल्ली भेजा ताकि मैं अच्छी शिक्षा प्राप्त कर सकू|

अपनी स्कूली शिक्षा पूरी करके मैंने दिल्ली विश्वविधालय से डिप्लोमा इन फार्मेसी किया| उसके बाद मैं आगे की पड़े फार्मेसी (ग्रेजुएशन एवं पोस्ट--ग्रेजुएशन) करना चाहता था १९९५ में फार्मेसी कालेज उतरी भारत बहुत काम थे | मेरे एक सम्बन्ध उनदिनों महाराष्ट्र के धूलिआ जिला में थे | प्रख्यात डॉ. डी.न वर्मा का परिवार वहाँ रहते है | रिश्ते में मेरी मामी डॉ. मृदुला वर्मा हिंदी साहित्ये की प्रख्यात विद्वान है वह वो एक कालेज में प्रोफेसर थी | उनके सहयोग से मैंने धूलिआ जिला के शिरपुर के एक कॉलेज में बी.फार्मा में दाखिला लिया | धूलिआ हमारे घर से बहुत दूर था इसके बावजूद मेरे पापा ने मुझे वह पढ़ने देने की इज़ाज़त दी और वे खुद मेरे साथ गए| क्योंकि कालेज का फी थोड़ा ज्यादा था वे थोड़ा चिंतित थे क्योंकि उनके ऊपर घर और समाज की जिम्मेवारियाँ भी थी

उनके जीवन की मुख्य उपलब्धियाँ

बालिका शिक्षा एवं महिला सशक्तिकरण

"एक अनुमान के तौर पर पिछले 40 वर्षो में, उनके अकेले प्रयासों और लगातार मदद के कारण 50 से अधिक छात्राएं सरकारी स्कूल में शिक्षक बनी।

उनकी कोशिश रहती थी की कि लड़कियों को स्कूल जाने के लिए लड़कों के समान ही अवसर मिले। उनका मानना था कि जब लड़कियों को शिक्षा मिलती है, तो इससे न केवल उनके परिवार बल्कि पुरा समाज सशक्त एवं सक्षम बनता है। ऐसे समाज में जहां शिक्षा के मामले में लड़कों और लड़कियों के साथ एक जैसा व्यवहार नहीं किया जाता था, उन्होंने लड़कियों की शिक्षा का समर्थन करने के लिए बहुत से प्रयास किये। उनका दृढ़ विश्वास था कि शिक्षा के माध्यम से महिलाओं को सशक्त बनाना सामाजिक प्रगति की कुंजी है।इसका जीता जगता उदहारण मेरी अम्माँ थीं|

1970 और 1980 में बिहार में लड़कियों की साक्षरता दर बहुत कम (8-10%) थी, बहुत सी लड़कियाँ स्कूल नहीं जाती थीं। सामाजिक बाधाएँ और कम उम्र में विवाह के कारण लड़कियों के लिए स्कूल जाना कठिन था। पापा उनके माता-पिता को मनाने और उनके बच्चियों का स्कूल में प्रवेश दिलाने में मदद करने, और हर सम्भव प्रयास करना उन्हें पढ़ाई के लिए प्रेरित करने की । और यदि तभी कोई माता पिता नहीं मानते थे तो उन्हें बहुत दुःख होता था कई बार घर पर वो उनका अफ़सोस प्रगट करते थे।

"उस ज़माने में लड़कियाँ सिर्फ खाना बनाती थीं चूल्हा चौका करती थी और घर का काम करती थीं, उन्होंने मुझे पढ़ाया और टीचिंग ट्रेनिंग कॉलेज में एडमिशन दिलवाया।

परिणामस्वरूप, मुझे 1975 में एक शिक्षक के रूप में नौकरी मिल गई। एक शिक्षित माँ होने के नाते, मैंने अपने 2 बेटों और 1 बेटी को खुद पढ़ाया। मेरे पति के आकस्मिक निधन के बाद, मेरी नौकरी ने मेरे जीवन और परिवार को आर्थिक रूप से मजबूत बनाए रखा, अन्यथा, आज हम सभी सड़कों पर रहते" - श्रीमती आशा सिन्हा, सेवानिवृत्त. स्कूल शिक्षक।

Fig 12 पापा अपने शिक्षकों के साथ, जिन्हें उन्होंने एक छात्र के रूप में भी पढ़ाया था

कुछ बालिकाओ या महिलाये को स्कूल जाने में परेशानी होती थी उनके लिए वो अपने घर पर भी पढ़ाने के इंतज़ाम किया| शाम को महिलाओं को उनके घरों में और उनके परिवारों के सामने ही पढ़ाया और शिक्षा दी। कुछ लोग हमारे घर लालटेन लेकर भी आते थे शाम को क्योंकि बिजली नहीं होती थी । उनकी शिक्षण शैली उत्कृष्ट एवं और बहुत ही अच्छी थी इस बात को ज्यादातर लोगो ने मुझसे साझा किया | हलाकि मैं भी उनका ही छात्र था । लोग उन पर इतना भरोसा करते थे कि बहुत लोगो ने अपने घर की महिलाओं को उनसे पढ़ने के लिए नहीं रोका । वे उसे एक विश्वसनीय व्यक्ति के रूप में जाने जाने लगे थे गांव में|

"मैं शाम को सर से सबक लेने आती थी, क्योंकि दिन में मुझे घर से बाहर जाने की इजाज़त नहीं थी। उन्होंने सभी कागजी कार्रवाई पूरी करवाई ताकि मैं एक प्राइवेट कैंडिडेट (उम्मीदवार) के रूप में 10वीं बोर्ड में शामिल हो सकूं। उन्हीं की वजह से मुझे बाद में शिक्षक प्रशिक्षण महाविद्यालय में दाखिला मिल गया और परिणामस्वरूप बाद में सरकारी शिक्षक की नौकरी के लिए चयनित हो गई" महिला छात्रा।

पापा के लिए महिला सशक्तिकरण सिर्फ एक नारा नहीं था। वह वास्तव में इस कहावत में विश्वास करते थे कि "दान घर से शुरू होता है" और वह इस पर कायम रहे। अम्मा एक अध्यापिका थीं, पापा से तीन साल पहले उन्होंने ज्वाइन किया था। वह पहले से ही हमारे परिवार में लड़कियों की शिक्षा का एक जीवंत उदाहरण थीं। पापा और अम्मा दोनों ने यह सुनिश्चित किया कि मेरी सभी मौसी और मेरी फुआ शिक्षा प्राप्त करें और आर्थिक रूप से स्वतंत्र हों। परिणामस्वरूप, मेरी तीन मौसी और एक फुआ, सरकारी स्कूलों में शिक्षक बने मेरे एक चाचा भी अपनी पढ़ाई पूरी करने के बाद शिक्षक बन गये।

उन्होंने महिलाओं की स्थिति को ऊपर उठाने और सामाजिक बाधाओं की जंजीरों को तोड़ने में शिक्षा की परिवर्तनकारी शक्ति को पहचाना। अपनी छात्राओं में आत्मविश्वास, स्वतंत्रता और महत्वाकांक्षा की भावना पैदा करके, उन्होंने एक ऐसे भविष्य के लिए बीज बोए जहाँ महिलाएँ जीवन के सभी क्षेत्रों में सक्रिय रूप से भाग ले सकें और योगदान दे सकें।

"मैं बहुत ही गरीब परिवार से हूँ | मेरी शादी बहुत कम उम्र हो गयी और मेरे दो बच्चे होने बाद अचानक ही मेरी पति की मित्र्यु हो गयी | मैं अपने माँ के यहाँ सोनपुर आ गई | मेरी माँ के कहने पर मास्टर साहेब ने मुझे 10 की पढ़ाई कराई | जिसके आधार पर उन्होंने बहुत प्रयास से मुझे आंगनवाड़ी में सेविका के रूप में

नौकरी दिलाने में बहुत बहुत मदद की उनके मदद के बिना इस गरीब कमजोर का काम नहीं हो पता| आज मैं अपने दो बच्चो को बड़ा करके पढ़ाई लिखाई करा के अपने पैरो को खड़ी हूँ" श्रीमती इंदु देवी, आंगनवाड़ी सेविका

> वह स्कूल के पक बन गए। जो वर्तमान में माध्यमिक कन्या विद्यालय के नाम से सुचारू रूप से चल रहा है, यह विद्यालय उस समय हरिहर क्षेत्र का पहला कन्या मध्य विद्यालय रहा होगा। महिला सशक्तिकरण में यह स्कूल अभूतपूर्व है।" श्री अजीत कुमार सिन्हा

उन वर्षों में, इंटरनेट और प्रौद्योगिकी के आगमन से पहले, अधिकांश कागजी काम मैन्युअल रूप से किए जाते थे। 10वीं कक्षा का बोर्ड फॉर्म प्राप्त करना, उसे हाथ से भरना, जिला कार्यालय में जमा करना, प्रवेश पत्र एकत्र करना और परीक्षा में शामिल होना जैसे काम सभी मैन्युअल प्रक्रियाओं के माध्यम से किए जाते थे। नौकरी आवेदन के लिए प्रमाणपत्रों को सत्यापित करना बहुत ही कठिन कार्य था। एक शिक्षक प्रशिक्षण स्कूल में प्रवेश सुरक्षित करने और पटना में शिक्षा विभाग से नियुक्तियाँ प्राप्त करने के लिए कई कदमों और निरंतर प्रयासों की आवश्यकता होती थी, वे शिक्षा से सम्बन्धिक काम के लिए कभी किसी को मना नहीं करते थे।

उन्होंने कभी भी अपने परिवार और दूसरों के बीच कोई भेद नहीं किया। उन्होंने बिना किसी भेदभाव के हर उस व्यक्ति की मदद की जो उनकी मदद के लिए उनके पास आते थे । बिहार में जातिप्रथा होने के बावजूद उन्होंने कभी भी जातीय के आधार पर कभी किसी को छोटा नहीं समझा | उसके पास सभी जाति के लोग आते थे वह सभी का काम करते थे| अध्यापन के अतिरिक्त ये सभी अतिरिक्त गतिविधियाँ उसे सुबह से देर शाम तक व्यस्त रखती थीं। एक लड़की और उसके माता-पिता के लिए, जो प्रक्रिया से अंजान थे, 10वीं बोर्ड परीक्षा का फॉर्म भरना और परीक्षा मैं बैठने, शिक्षक प्रशिक्षण स्कूल में प्रवेश पाना और सरकारी शिक्षक के रूप में नौकरी सुरक्षित करना लगभग असंभव था। ऐसे चुनौतीपूर्ण समय के दौरान, उन्होंने व्यक्तिगत बिना अपने समय की परवाह

किये सदा मदद के लिए तैयार रहते थे और शिक्षा से लेकर बोर्ड परीक्षा, शिक्षक प्रशिक्षण स्कूल में प्रवेश, स्कूल में नियुक्ति तक पूरी प्रक्रिया के हर कदम पर मदद प्रदान की। वे अक्सर जिला शिक्षा कार्यालय और राजधानी पटना में शिक्षा विभाग का किसी न किसी के शिक्षा सम्बंधित कार्य के लिए जाते रहते थे। 30-40 वर्षों तक, प्रत्येक वर्ष, उन्होंने अनगिनत छात्रों को अथक रूप से इस प्रकार की सहायता प्रदान की।

> "उनके लिए, उनके परिवार की सीमाएँ बहुत बड़ी थीं, जो कोई भी उनके पास आता था, वे उनके साथ अपने परिवार के सदस्य की तरह व्यवहार करते थे और उनकी मदद करते थे। अक्सर, हमने देखा है कि लोग (शिक्षक या माता-पिता या छात्र) शिक्षण संबंधी कार्यों के लिए सुबह 5 बजे के आसपास "मास्टर साब या सर" से मिलने के लिए हमारे घर आने लगते। "श्रीमती अल्पना सिन्हा (देजी दीदी) और श्रीमती रश्मी सिन्हा (दीदी-बहन)।

उनका मानना था कि शिक्षा किसी के जीवन में बड़ा बदलाव ला सकती है, जिससे उन्हें समाज की सीमा और बंधनो से मुक्त होने में मदद मिलेगी।

उन्होंने अपनी छात्राओं को आत्मविश्वासी, स्वतंत्र और महत्वाकांक्षी बनने के लिए प्रोत्साहित किया। वह चाहते थे कि उनका भविष्य उज्ज्वल हो जहाँ वे जीवन की हर चीज़ में हिस्सा ले सकें। हमारे समुदाय में, हमने देखा है कि जब महिलाओं को अच्छी नौकरियाँ मिलती हैं, जैसे शिक्षक बनना या सरकार के लिए काम करना तो चीजें कैसे बदल जाती हैं। उनके परिवार आर्थिक रूप से सबल हो जाते है और उनके बच्चों को अच्छी शिक्षा मिलती है।

यहां तक कि जिन लोगों ने जॉब के बजाये गृहथी संभाला, उन पर भी सकारात्मक प्रभाव पड़ा। उन्होंने बच्चों को अच्छी शिक्षा दी । इसलिए, मेरे पापा के प्रयासों की बदौलत, बहुत से परिवार के जीवन में बेहतर बदलाव आया|

पेशेवर ज़िंदगी

एक समय की बात है, उन्होंने सोनपुर के तीन ब्लॉकों (तहसील) के मध्य विद्यालयों में शिक्षकों के वेतन और भुगतान का प्रबंधन किया। उन वर्षों में, प्रधानाध्यापक शिक्षकों का वेतन तैयार करने और उसे राजकोष में जमा करने के लिए जिम्मेदार होते थे। कई स्कूलों में प्रधानाध्यापकों की नहीं होने के कारण, उन्होंने उन स्कूलों में 100 से अधिक शिक्षकों के वेतन डेटा को संकलित करने के लिए अकेले काम किया।

उनके पेशेवर जीवन में विभिन्न पहलू शामिल थे। उन्होंने कई वर्षों तक प्राथमिक शिक्षक संघ के अध्यक्ष के रूप में कार्य किया। इसके अतिरिक्त, उन्होंने छात्रों से जुड़ी पाठ्येतर गतिविधियों, जैसे संगीत कार्यक्रमों और स्कूल समारोहों के उत्सव में सक्रिय रूप से भाग लिया।

एक उल्लेखनीय घटना में, लगभग 72 वर्ष की आयु में, ग्रामीणों ने उन्हें कोषाध्यक्ष नियुक्त करते हुए, वार्षिक दुर्गा पूजा कार्यक्रम आयोजित करने का अनुरोध किया। यह सबसे यादगार घटनाओं में से एक साबित हुई क्योंकि लोगों ने उन पर भरोसा किया, जिसके परिणामस्वरूप हर वर्ष से ज्यादा दान मिला। सभी खर्चों के बाद, वह लगभग 2 लाख रुपये बचाने में सफल रहे, जिसका उपयोग अगले वर्ष में किया गया।

सेवानिवृत्ति के बाद का जीवन

Fig 14. बरबट्टा स्कूल में सेवानिवृत्ति समारोह सोनपुर (2002)

ऐसे कम ही लोग होते हैं जो रिटायरमेंट के बाद अपने पेशे से काफी सक्रियता से जुड़े रहते हैं। शिक्षा एक ऐसा पेशा है जो आपको ऐसा मौका देता है कि आप अपने पेशे से जुड़े रहे| पापा भी अपने पेशे से जुड़े रहे| हालाँकि, शिक्षा के प्रति उनकी प्रतिबद्धता की कोई सीमा नहीं थी। सेवानिवृत्ति के बाद उनके जीवन में एक नया अध्याय जुड़ा, जहाँ वे तीसरी और चौथी पीढ़ी के लिए एक मार्गदर्शक के रूप में काम करते रहे। शिक्षा के प्रति उनका जुनून कम नहीं हुआ और उन्होंने सीखने की प्रक्रिया में योगदान देने के लिए नए हमेशा तैयार रहे । सेवानिवृत्ति के 20 साल बाद भी, वह कई स्कूलों के छात्रों और शिक्षकों के साथ जुड़े हुए थे और शिक्षण, मार्गदर्शन और सलाह और शैक्षिक गतिविधियों में सक्रिय रूप से शामिल रहते थे। अधिकांश सेवानिवृत्त शिक्षकों को इतने लंबे समय के बाद स्कूल या छात्र याद नहीं रखते है, लेकिन पापा अलग थे उनको उनको तो २०२३ में परीक्षा देनेलाये विद्‌याथी भी जानते थे और उनसे पढ़ने आते थे । हमारे पहाड़ीचक गर्ल्स स्कूल के जो भी शिक्षक-शिक्षिकाएं को शिक्षा सम्बंधित कठिनाई आती थी वो पापा को याद करते थे| अक्सर, शिक्षकों की सेवानिवृत्ति और पेंशन संबंधी मामलों पर

उनकी राय, सुझाव और मदद के लिए उन्हें आसपास के कई स्कूलों के प्रधानाध्यापक या शिक्षकों के फोन आते थे।

> "दिन में जब भी मैंने उसे बेल्जियम से फोन किया, वह आमतौर पर हाई स्कूल होते थे । मैंने उससे पूछा कि वह घर पर अधिक आराम क्यों नहीं करते है, और उसने विनम्रता से कहा, "मुझे घर की तुलना में स्कूल में बैठना अधिक अच्छा लगता है।" - डॉ. गौरव कुमार (पुत्र)

वे सोनपुर छोड़कर ज्यादा दिन के लिए कही भी जाना पसंद नहीं करते थे जैसे सोनपुर में उनके प्राण बसते थे| मैंने उनसे कई बार आग्रह किया की वो थोड़ा समय हमारे साथ विदेश में आकर बिताये पर वे बोले की एक बार आएंगे विदेश देखने पर मेरा मन नहीं लगेगा वहाँ| हालांकि वे एक बार ऑस्ट्रेलिया आये और एक बार बेल्जियम |

इस उम्र में भी शैक्षणिक गतिविधियों के प्रति पापा की ऊर्जा और उत्साह अद्वितीय था। उनकी दिनचर्या में न केवल व्यक्तिगत चिंतन शामिल था बल्कि शैक्षिक गतिविधियों में सक्रिय भागीदारी भी शामिल थी। शिक्षा के प्रति उनकी स्थायी प्रतिबद्धता इस तथ्य का प्रमाण थी कि शिक्षण, उनके लिए सिर्फ एक पेशा नहीं बल्कि एक आजीवन कार्य था।

स्वास्थ्य के प्रति जागरूक

इतनी लम्बी आयु तक कैसे स्वस्थ और सक्रिय रहे वे हमसब के लिए एक प्रेरणा एवं मिशाल है| उनकी दिनचर्या सुबह 5 बजे से शुरू होती थी, रोजाना योग करके, सुबह की सैर, नाश्ते से पहले स्नान और पूजा करके अपने काम के लिए घर से निकलना। सालो तक उनका एक ही दिनचर्या था. वे सुबह उठने के पक्षधर थे हलाकि आजकल हमलोग देर से सोना और देर तक उठने प्रचलन हो गया है पर मैं जब भी सोनपुर आता था तो वे सुबह से ही आवाज लगाने लगते थे |

80 साल की उम्र में, जब उन्हें लगा कि साइकिल चलाना अधिक कठिन होता जा रहा है, तो उन्होंने सुझाव दिया कि मैं उनके लिए एक इलेक्ट्रिक साइकिल खरीदूं। नवंबर 2022 में, मैंने

उनके लिए एक इलेक्ट्रिक साइकिल ख़रीदा, और एक बच्चे के सामान वे हर दिन इसका उपयोग करने के लिए रोमांचित रहते थे। उन्होंने एक बार मुझसे कहा था, "मैं जहां भी जाता हूं, लोग इलेक्ट्रिक साइकिल देखने के लिए इकट्ठा हो जाते हैं भीड़ लग जाता है।"

> "मुझे याद है कि एक बार, 1997 में 44 साल की उम्र में, उनके दिल में थोड़ी समस्या हो गई थी। उन्होंने इसे नजरअंदाज के करने बजाय अपनी जीवन में कुछ बड़े बदलाव किए. उन्होंने अपनी मोटरसाइकिल चलाना बंद कर दिया और पहले की तरह हर दिन अपनी साइकिल का उपयोग करना शुरू कर दिए। दरअसल, बाद में वे मोटरसाइकिल सिर्फ अपने स्वास्थ्य कारणों से बेच दिए। वह अपने आखिरी दिन तक खूब साइकिल चलते रहे थे, कभी-कभी तो हर दिन 10-15 किलोमीटर तक। वे स्वस्थ के प्रति इतने सजग थे कि नियमित स्वास्थ्य जांच और रक्त परीक्षण करवाया करते थे।"

अभिभावक परिप्रेक्ष्य: प्रभावी शिक्षण के लिए मार्गदर्शन

मेरे माता-पिता ने कभी भी मुझ पर कोई विशिष्ट कैरियर मार्ग नहीं थोपा; इसके बजाय, उन्होंने मुझे अपनी विषय चुनने की आज़ादी दी। 12 साल की उम्र में, उन्होंने मुझे बेहतर शैक्षिक अवसरों के लिए दिल्ली में मेरे मामा के पास रहने के लिए भेज दिया। मैंने लगन से काम किया और अपनी परीक्षाओं में लगातार उत्कृष्ट प्रदर्शन किया। मैं मेडिकल डॉक्टर बनाना चाहता था पर 1994-1996 में मेडिकल परीक्षा बहुत कठिन थी, सरकारी मेडिकल कॉलेजेस कम थे तो सीटें भी कम थी, जिसके लिए लाखो छात्र परीक्षा में बैठते थे, कई प्रयास के बाद जब मेरा मेरिट लिस्ट में नाम नहीं आया तब मैंने फार्मेसी कॉलेज में दाखिला लिया क्योंकि फार्मेसी भी मेडिकल की तरह था। दिल्ली विश्वविद्यालय के अंतर्गत, मैंने योग्यता के आधार पर डिप्लोमा स्ट्रीम में एक प्रतिष्ठित फार्मेसी कॉलेज में प्रवेश प्राप्त किया। अपने डिप्लोमा अध्ययन के दौरान, मुझे वैज्ञानिक बनने की आकांक्षा के साथ फार्मेसी में आगे की शिक्षा प्राप्त करने में गहरी रुचि विकसित

हुई। इसके बाद, मैंने बी.फार्मा की डिग्री हासिल की और 97.3 प्रतिशत के साथ गेट परीक्षा पास कर छात्रवृत्ति के साथ पंजाब विश्वविद्यालय, चंडीगढ़ मास्टर इन फार्मेसी (M.Pharmacy) में प्रवेश प्राप्त किया। इस शैक्षिक यात्रा के दौरान, पापा ने लगातार मेरा समर्थन किया और मुझे सरकारी क्षेत्र में, विशेषकर फार्मासिस्ट के पदों के लिए आवेदन करने के लिए प्रोत्साहित करते रहे|

एक बार मैं रेलवे फार्मासिस्ट पद के लिए लिखित परीक्षा में उत्तीर्ण हो गया, लेकिन असफल साक्षात्कार का सामना करना पड़ा। अपनी मास्टर डिग्री पूरी करने के बाद, मैंने 2003 में इंदौर के एक प्रतिष्ठित सरकारी संस्थान में फार्मेसी विभाग में व्याख्याता के रूप में एक पद हासिल किया। पापा इस उपलब्धि से बहुत खुश हुए, कि मैं उनसे एक कदम आगे निकल गया हूँ | वे बहुत गौरवान्वित होकर कहते थे की मेरे बेटे का पे-स्केल (pay scale) मेरे रिटायरमेंट के समय के पे स्केल (pay scale) से भी ज्यादा है।

Fig 15 व्याख्याता के रूप में कार्यभार ग्रहण करने के समय

अपनी सफलता के बावजूद, मेरे मन में एक वैज्ञानिक के रूप में अपना करियर बनाने की इच्छा थी, मेरा लक्ष्य अनुसंधान और पीएच.डी. करना था। मैं विदेश से एक प्रतिष्ठित विश्वविद्यालय में पीएचडी करना चाहता था । सौभाग्य से, मुझे ऑस्ट्रेलिया में एक

अवसर मिला। हालाँकि पापा मेरी उपलब्धियों से खुश थे, लेकिन वे मेरे व्याख्याता पद से इस्तीफा देने के मेरे फैसले से सहमत नहीं थे पर उन्होंने कभी रोका या टोका नहीं| हमेशा यही कहते थे ठीक से देख समझ ले जो ठीक लगे.

मैं 2003 में फार्मेसी विभाग में एक व्याख्याता के रूप में पढ़ना शुरू किया तो मुझे नहीं पता था की कैसे क्लास ली जाती है| मैं अपने विषय की किताब लेकर जाता था और किताब से देखकर पढ़ता था. जब पापा ने मुझसे लेक्चर की तैयारी के बारे में पूछा तो मैंने किताब देखकर पढ़ने वाली बात कही। उन्होंने फिर मुझे समझया की कैसे क्लास की तयारी पहले से करते है है. उन्होंने एक बात बोली की कम से कम मुझे रोज 1-2 घण्टे अपना लेक्चर तैयार करने पर बीतता चाहिए और क्लास में कब क्या पढ़ना है उनकी प्लानिंग करनी चाहिए | तब मुझे पता चला की लेक्चर कैसे तैयार करते हैं. एक दिलचस्प कक्षा वातावरण बनाने पर बहुमूल्य सुझाव दिए। परिणामस्वरूप, मेरा शिक्षण अत्यधिक प्रभावी हो गया, मैं भी अपने डिपार्टमेंट में छात्रों के बीच बहुत चर्तित और मिलनसार शिक्षक के रूप में जानेजाने लगा | कई छात्रों ने मेरा विषय फार्माकोलॉजी में का चयन किया आगे जाकर पढ़ाई की । कुछ लोग ऑस्ट्रेलिया, अमेरिका और ब्रिटेन के शीर्ष संस्थानों में अग्रणी वैज्ञानिक बन गए हैं।

समापन अभ्युक्ति:

उनके बेटे के रूप में, मैं एक पुस्तक के माध्यम से उनके जीवन के कार्यों को अमर बनाने की अंतर्निहित जिम्मेदारी महसूस करता हूं। यह प्रयास केवल घटनाओं के पुनर्गणना से आगे जाता है; यह उस महान व्यक्तित्व को श्रद्धांजलि है जिन्होंने अपना पूरा जीवन एक नेक काम के लिए समर्पित कर दिया। पुस्तक का उद्देश्य उनकी शिक्षाओं का सार, उनके छात्रों के जीवन में परिवर्तनकारी क्षण, महिला सशक्तीकरण और उनकी अटूट प्रतिबद्धता के माध्यम से उनके द्वारा किए गए सामाजिक परिवर्तनों को शामिल करना है।

मैं भावी पीढ़ियों को एक समर्पित शिक्षक के समाज पर पड़ने वाले गहरे प्रभाव को पहचानने के लिए प्रेरित करना चाहता हूँ। पापा का जीवन एक प्रकाशस्तंभ के रूप हमें ऐसे भविष्य की ओर

मार्गदर्शन करता है जहां शिक्षा केवल ज्ञान प्राप्त करने का साधन नहीं है बल्कि सकारात्मक परिवर्तन, सशक्तिकरण और सामाजिक प्रगति के लिए उत्प्रेरक है।

जब मैं अपनी पीएचडी के दौरान ऑस्ट्रेलिया में था, तो मैं अपने माता-पिता को विदेश घुमाना चाहता था । किसी तरह उन्हें मना लिया गया और वीजा मिल गया। वह संभवतः सिंगापुर या मलेशिया एयरलाइंस (मुझे ठीक से याद नहीं है) वे, मेरी पत्नी और कुछ महीने के बेटे यश के साथ मेलबर्न की पहली विदेश यात्रा किये । यह एक उल्लेखनीय यात्रा थी. उन्होंने मेलबर्न शहर का पैदल भ्रमण किया, प्रतिदिन कई किलोमीटर पैदल चलते रहते थे और कई घंटों तक हर चीज़ का ध्यानपूर्वक अवलोकन करते रहते थे।

Fig 16a - पहली उड़ान और पहली विदेश यात्रा मेरी पत्नी और कुछ महीने के बेटे यश के साथ मेलबर्न हवाई अड्डे पर (2008)

बाद में जब मैं बेल्जियम चला गया तो मैं चाहता था कि वह यहां भी आएं। चूँकि बेल्जियम में आधिकारिक भाषाएँ डच और फ्रेंच हैं, और मेरा बेटा डच बोलता है, इसलिए उन्होंने डच सीखना शुरू कर दिए । पुरे शहर पैदल ही घूम लिए| हर रोज वे एक दिशा में जाते थे| उन्होंने कुछ ऐसी बाते बताई जो हमें पता ही नहीं थी, हमने अभी तक नहीं देखा था।

Fig 16b मेलबर्न में "द ट्वेल्व एपोस्टल्स" का दौरा

अभिस्वीकृति (आभार)

इस पुस्तक के माध्यम से, मैं उन सभी के प्रति अपनी गहरी भावनात्मक कृतज्ञता व्यक्त करना चाहता हूं जिन्होंने इस चुनौतीपूर्ण समय के दौरान निस्वार्थ रूप से मेरा साथ और सहयोग दिया | पापा की मृत्यु के बाद अगले 15 दिनों, मुझे - परिवार के सदस्यों, रिश्तेदारों, पड़ोसियों, ग्रामीणों, शिक्षकों, उनके पूर्व सहयोगियों और दोस्तों भरपूर सहयोग मिला । पिछला एक साल मेरे लिए भावनात्मक रूप से चुनौतीपूर्ण और मुश्किल भरा समय था, और मैं कुछ व्यक्तियों को उनके असाधारण भावनात्मक और सहयोग के लिए धन्यवाद देना चाहता हूं|

मैं पापा को अचानक खोने के लिए मानसिक रूप से तैयार नहीं था। मैं भारत में परिवार की सभी चिंताओं से दूर बेल्जियम रह रहा था | पापा के होते मुझे कभी कुछ चिंता करने की जरूरत ही नहीं पड़ी | मैंने कभी सपने में भी नहीं सोचा था कि अचानक ऐसा वक्त आ जायेगा । सुबह-सुबह जब मैंने यह खबर सुनी तो मेरे होश उड़ गए, मेरी आवाज रुंध गई। हालांकि मैं खुद को मजबूत करने की कोशिश कर रहा था और अपने आंसुओं को रोक रहा था, लेकिन जब विजय ने मुझे एयरपोर्ट पर छोड़ा, तो फ्लाइट में मेरे आंसू नहीं रुक रहे थे| मेरे जीवन की सबसे कठिन यात्रा थी पटना एयरपोर्ट से उतरने के बाद घर पहुंचने तक का, मैं सोच भी नहीं पा रहा था कि मैं खुद को कैसे संभालूंगा। पहुंचने के बाद मैं पापा के गले लगकर फूट-फूट कर रोने लगा, हालांकि जल्द ही मैंने अम्मा, बहनों और रिश्तेदारों की हालत देखी कि वे कितने भावुक हो गए थे, मैं उसके बाद किसी के सामने नहीं रोया ।

मैं देजी दीदी, कमकम दीदी और छोटे जीजा जी को हृदय से धन्यवाद और आभार व्यक्त करता हूं। वे तीनों अम्मा का जीवन बचाने के लिए क्योंकि की उनकी भी हालत बहुत ज्यादा ख़राब थी दिन रात लगे थे । मैं बेहद चिंतित था कि कहीं अम्मा की बिगड़ती हालत को देखते हुए मैं उन्हें खो न दूं, क्योंकि उन्होंने कई दिनों से पानी या भोजन की एक बूंद भी नहीं ली है। वे दैनिक अनुष्ठानों में मेरा साथ दे रहे थे और भावनात्मक रूप से एक-दूसरे का साथ दे रहे थे। मेरी पत्नी अर्चना सुख-दुख की साथी है और समझती है कि मुझे क्या चाहिए और मैं कैसे सोचता हूं। विकसित देशों में 18 साल से अधिक समय बिताने के बाद सोनपुर में रहना मेरे लिए बेहद कठिन था, लेकिन मेरी स्थिति को समझा मेरा पूरा सहयोग और साथ दी । वह अकेले बेल्जियम में मेरी ज़िम्मेदारियों की देखभाल करने में एक चैंपियन है । छोटे पापा (श्री मदन मोहन प्रसाद), बड़े मामा (श्री अजित कुमार सिन्हा), छोटे भैया (श्री हेमन्तचन्द्र वर्मा, मधेपुरा) मेरे और मेरे लिए परिवार के तीन मजबूत स्तंभों की तरह थे। उन्होंने मुझे और मेरे परिवार को कभी भी 15-20 दिनों तक अकेला नहीं छोड़ा। जब तक घर की सभी रस्में और संबंधित काम पूरे नहीं हो गए, उसके बाद ही वे अपने काम और घर के लिए निकले। वे मेरी ज़रूरत के हर पल के लिए मेरे लिए मौजूद थे। मनोज मामा और संजय भैया प्यार और स्नेह के 2 रत्नों की तरह थे, मेरे लिए उनका भावनात्मक लगाव और देखभाल मेरे लिए अविस्मरणीय थी। विजय लंबे समय से मेरा सबसे अच्छा दोस्त रहा है, मैं उस पर आंख मूंदकर भरोसा करता हूं। जब मैंने अपने पापा की मृत्यु के बारे में सुना तो कुछ ही मिनटों में मैंने उन्हें सुबह-सुबह फोन किया। वह आए और मेरी तात्कालिक जरूरतों और भावनात्मक सहयोग का ख्याल रखा, क्योंकि अचानक ऐसी खबरें सुनने के बाद मेरा दिमाग ठीक से काम नहीं कर रहा था। लगभग 2 महीने तक बेल्जियम में मेरी अनुपस्थिति में, मैं उस पर भरोसा कर सकता था। धनंजय भैया (मेरे पड़ोसी श्री धनंजय सिंह) मेरे पापा की मृत्यु के बाद बहुत चिंतित थे, उन्होंने वास्तव में एक अभिभावक की तरह काम किया और मुझे इतना प्यार भरी देखभाल और सहयोग दिया कि मुझे

विश्वास हो गया कि मैं गाँव में अकेला नहीं रह गया हूँ। श्री अजय कुमार सिंह (नुन्नु) भैया) को अनुष्ठान गतिविधियों की निगरानी में उनके मदद के लिए धन्यवाद। यश बहुत छोटा है, लेकिन यह बहुत राहत की बात थी कि वह स्थिति को समझता था, जब वह यहां सोनपुर आया, तो वह परिवार और बच्चों के साथ अच्छी तरह से घुलमिल गया, जल्दी ही 60-70 लोगों के साथ घर में, जिससे मुझे कभी चिंता महसूस नहीं हुई। मेरे जीवन के ये सभी नायक, हर कदम पर उनका अटूट समर्थन इतना था कि मुझे पहले महीने और उसके बाद दबाव और तनाव महसूस नहीं हुआ। वे मेरे जीवन में मजबूत स्तंभों की तरह थे।' इस कठिन समय में मैंने पहले कभी अपने परिवार में इतना मजबूत अनुभव नहीं किया था।

सभी अंतिम संस्कार और अनुष्ठान सुचारू रूप से आयोजित किए गए, और अनुष्ठानों के बाद, मैं भारत में अपने परिवार और बेल्जियम में घर दोनों को समान रूप से अच्छी तरह से प्रबंधित करने में सक्षम था।

मैं विशेष रूप से छोटे पापा और बड़े मामा को इस पुस्तक की निरंतर चर्चा, लेखन और प्रारूपण के लिए धन्यवाद देता हूं। वे नियमित रूप से मुझे मेरे पापा के जीवन के बारे में इनपुट और बहुमूल्य जानकारी प्रदान करते रहे। इस पुस्तक को पूरा करने में उनका योगदान महत्वपूर्ण है। उन सभी को धन्यवाद जिन्होंने पापा के साथ अपने अनुभव लिखने के लिए समय निकाला। पिछले वर्षों में गाँव में बड़े भाई के रूप में मेरा लगातार समर्थन करने और सहयोग लिए गुल्लू भैया (श्री राकेश राज सिंह) और इस पुस्तक की तैयारी में बंटू (सीमांत सिंह गौतम) को धन्यवाद।

उमेश ठाकुर जो हमारे घर के सारे छोटे मोटे काम से लेकर सभी अनुष्ठान में दिन रात काम किया बहुत ही धन्यवाद् उसका. उसका भी मेरे पापा के प्रति बहुत प्रेम था. ललिता की माँ जो हमरे घर पर काम करती है वो भी बहुत लगन से बिना किसी शिकायत के दिन रात हमलोग के जरुरत का ध्यान रखने के लिए धन्यवाद् और प्रणाम

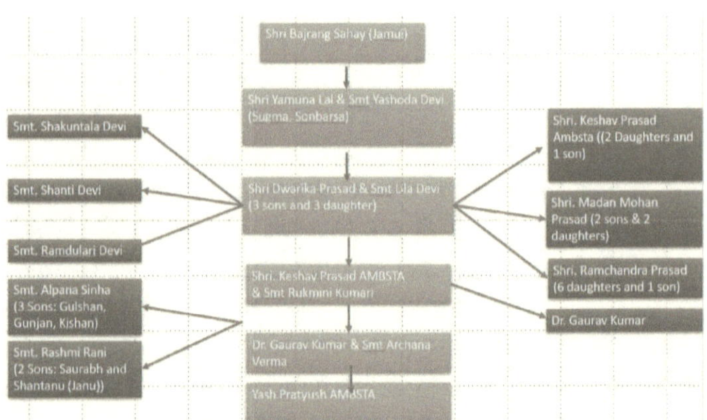

Shri Bajrang Sahay (Jamui)
Shri Yamuna Lal & Smt Yashoda Devi (Sugma, Sonbarsa)
Shri Dwarika Prasad & Smt Lila Devi (3 sons and 3 daughter)
Shri. Keshav Prasad AMBSTA & Smt Rukmini Kumari
Dr. Gaurav Kumar & Smt Archana Verma
Yash Pratyush AMBSTA
Smt. Shakuntala Devi
Smt. Shanti Devi
Smt. Ramdulari Devi
Smt. Alpana Sinha (3 Sons: Gulshan, Gunjan, Kishan)
Smt. Rashmi Rani (2 Sons: Saurabh and Shantanu (Janu))
Shri. Keshav Prasad Ambsta ((2 Daughters and 1 son)
Shri. Madan Mohan Prasad (2 sons & 2 daughters)
Shri. Ramchandra Prasad (6 daughters and 1 son)
Dr. Gaurav Kumar

Fig 16c. वंशावली

लोगों का अनुभव

श्रीमती आशा सिन्हा (आशा मौसी) - सेवानिवृत्त मध्य विद्यालय, शिक्षिका, छपरा

अश्वनी कुमार (मोनू), छपरा - बीपीएससी उत्तीर्ण 10-12वीं कक्षा के शिक्षक, सरकारी स्कूल, छपरा

मौसा जी, जिन्हें हम सभी प्यार से बड़का मौसा कहते थे। वे केवल नाम के बड़े नहीं थे बल्कि उन्होंने बड़े होने के सभी दायित्व का निर्वहन भी किया है। हमारे परिवार (ननिहाल) में शायद ही कोई ऐसा होगा जिनके जीवन में मौसा जी का कोई न कोई अहम योगदान न रहा हो। जैसा कि मेरी मम्मी भी कहती है कि जिस जमाने में लड़कियां केवल चूल्हा- चौका करती थी, उस जमाने में बड़का मेहमान हम लोगों को सोनपुर में पढ़ने - लिखने का अवसर प्रदान करने में सहायक रहे तथा शिक्षक प्रशिक्षण महाविद्यालय में दाखिला करवाया फलस्वरूप शिक्षक की नौकरी मिली वरना आज हम सभी सड़क पर रहते। मौसाजी के लिए परिवार का दायरा बहुत ही विशाल था । आज जहाँ लोग थोड़े में ही सिमटकर रहना पसंद करते हैं वही मौसाजी, हर एक सगे संबंधी और जो भी उनके संपर्क में रहा उनके परिवार का हिस्सा हो जाता था। किसी के भी सुख-दुख में हर प्रकार से उपस्थित रहने में उन्हें तनिक भी हिचकिचाहट न थी । स्वयं मेरा संबंध अपने चचेरे भाईयों और चाची के साथ अच्छा नहीं रहा है, परंतु आज उन लोगों के साथ में हम सभी का संबंध अच्छा है। इस सुधार में भी मौसा जी की अहम भूमिका रही है।आज के दौर में जहाँ किसी से पैसा तो दूर की बात है, अगर समय पर कोई सलाह भी मांगी जाए तो अधिकतर लोग गलत सलाह ही देंगे, जबकि मौसाजी सभी के लिए चाहे बात पैसे की हो, शारीरिक हो, कागजी हो, पैरवी हो या कोई सलाह ही हो हर प्रकार से मैंने उन्हें खड़ा पाया है। जिसने भी उनसे अगर दूरी बनाई है वह स्वयं नुकसान में रहा है । वे सकारात्मक ऊर्जा के भंडार थे। मौसाजी के साथ मुझे सोनपुर - हाजीपुर घूमने का अवसर मिला है। मैंने देखा है कि शायद ही कोई

होगा जो आपको न जानता हो। सभी से प्रेमपूर्वक मिलना-जुलना, बात करना, लोगों को ध्यानपूर्वक सुनना उनकी खूबी थी। समस्या चाहे जितनी भी बड़ी हो वे सहज भाव से कहते थे "कोई बात नहीं, सब ठीक हो जाएगा" । बड़ी सी बड़ी समस्या होने पर जहाँ लोग सिर पीटने लगते हैं उस समय पर भी मौसा जी शांत रहा करते थे। वे बहुत विशेष परिस्थिति में ही किसी की कड़वी बातों की प्रतिक्रिया देते थे, वरना शांति से विवाद को समाप्त कर देते थे। वो हमेशा आस-पास के लोगों को आपसी विवाद, कड़वाहट को दूर करने के लिए प्रेरित करते थे।

सरकारी शिक्षक की नौकरी तो बहुत से लोग करते हैं, जो 6 घंटे की ड्यूटी करके सीधे घर आकर अपने परिवार तक सीमित रहते हैं लेकिन हमारे मौसा जी ऐसा बिल्कुल न थे। सरकारी सेवा में रहते हुए सामाजिक कार्यों, सार्वजनिक पूजा-पाठ इत्यादि कार्यों में व्यस्त रहा करते थे। सेवानिवृत्ति के उपरांत भी वे सदा शिक्षण संबंधी कार्यों में संलग्न रहा करते थे। मौसाजी की सबसे बड़ी खूबी यह थी कि वे हमेशा लोगों को पढ़ाई, प्रतियोगी परीक्षा के लिए प्रेरित किया करते थे। उनके मुख से कभी भी नकारात्मक बात नहीं निकलती थी। एक बार मैंने मौसा जी से कहा भी था कि "मौसा जी मैं सिर्फ और दो वर्ष प्रतियोगी परीक्षाओं के लिए प्रयास करूँगा अब चाहे सरकारी जॉब मिले या ना मिले"। इस पर मौसा जी ने कहा कि "नहीं ऐसा नहीं कहो और 2 साल नहीं इसके भीतर ही तुम्हारा हो जाएगा"। इस बीच मौसा जी चल बसे और मौसा जी के आशीर्वचनों के परिणाम स्वरूप मेरे कई प्रतियोगी परीक्षाओं के परिणाम आये तथा कई परीक्षाओं में सफलता रहा । इन्हीं एक-डेढ़ वर्षों के भीतर बीपीएससी द्वारा आयोजित शिक्षक भर्ती परीक्षा प्रथम प्रयास में उत्तीर्ण हुआ और कक्षा ग्यारहवीं-बारहवीं के लिए चयनीत हुआ। अफसोस है कि आज मौसा जी हमारे बीच नहीं रहे, लेकिन इस सुखद परिणाम के प्रेरणा स्रोत मौसा जी ही रहे है। मौसा जी ने अपना संपूर्ण जीवन, पठन-पाठन, महिला शिक्षा, अन्य सामाजिक एवं सार्वजनिक कार्यों को समर्पित कर दिया था । आज भले आप सशरीर हमारे बीच नहीं हैं परंतु आपके द्वारा दिए गए हैं सीख और मार्गदर्शन के रूप में सदा हमारे बीच रहेंगे।

श्री हेम चन्द्र वर्मा

"जीवन की अब अनियंत्रित ऊर्जा को।नियंत्रित कर जीवन को सही दिशा सवस्थ जीवन, लंबी उम्र एवं सफलताओं का अंबार लगाने की दिशा में अग्रसर रहने के लिए वे प्रेरित करते थे। और वे घर, परिवार से लेकर समाज, कस्बे के बच्चे, बच्ची, युवति, युवकों को शिक्षा के लिए हमेशा चलते फिरते प्रोत्साहित करते रहते थे और जीवन के अंतिम क्षण तक वे शिक्षा का दान देते रहे।

वह एक योग प्रधानाध्यापक के साथ बड़े ही कुशल एवं बेहतरीन अभिभावक भी थे।जिनके सफल एवं कुशल नेतृत्व के कारण ही हमेशा कर्मानुसार हमलोग इतने आगे बढ़ते रहें। वे प्राथमिक विधयालय तुनियाही से चौथी एवं पांचवी कक्षा की पढ़ाई की, उसके बाद MPHS इंटरमीडिएट इंटर स्तरीय मल्टीपर्पस हायर सेकेंडरी विधयालय मधेपुरा से पूर्ण पढ़ाई करने के बाद आगे की पढ़ाई कॉलेज बेगूसराय एवं अन्य स्थानों से पूरी किया। बेगूसराय में महा विद्यालय में पढ़ाई करने के दौरान ही उनकी शादी बेगूसराय में संपन्न। सोनपुर में शिक्षा विभाग के संगठन के अधिकारी के रूप में वे कुशल नेतृत्व प्रदान किए।"

श्रीमती अल्पना सिन्हा, शिक्षिका, मध्य विद्यालय पहाड़ीचक, सोनपुर (बड़ी बहन)

मेरे पापा और मम्मी दोनों ने यह सुनिश्चित किया कि मैं शिक्षा प्राप्त करूँ और अपनी पढ़ाई अच्छे से करूँ। जब मैंने 10वीं प्रथम श्रेणी से उत्तीर्ण की, तो वह चाहते थे कि मैं प्रतियोगी परीक्षाओं की तैयारी करूँ। मेरी इच्छा स्कूल में अपनी माँ की तरह शिक्षक बनने की थी। इसलिए, मैंने शिक्षक प्रशिक्षण करना पसंद किया और फिर कुछ वर्षों के बाद मुझे सरकारी शिक्षक की नौकरी मिल गई। मेरे पिता अखबार और सामान्य ज्ञान पढ़ने के लिए बार-बार कहते रहते थे ताकि मैं बेहतर जानकारी प्राप्त कर सकूं और अपने छात्रों को अच्छे से पढ़ा सकूं। वह अपने अंतिम समय तक स्कूल के किसी भी प्रशासनिक काम में मेरी मदद के लिए मौजूद रहे।

आखिरी दिन, मैं सुबह 9 बजे स्कूल के लिए निकली, अपनी पानी की बोतल लेना भूल गयी। तो, उसने बोतल भर दी और घर मे का करने वाली से कहा कि इसे स्कूल भेज दो। वास्तव में, वह मेरा और किसी का भी बहुत ख्याल रखते थे

जब से मैंने होश सम्भाला है, पापा का रूटीन एक जैसा रहा है।5:00 बजे उठना, नित्य क्रिया के बाद नींबू पानी पीना। स्नान, पूजा जरूर करना बिस्कुट मेरी गोल्डन उनका फेवरेट बिस्कुट चाय पीना के साथ, ।पापा का रूटीन मुझे बहुत अच्छा लगता था। उनका घर चलाने का तरीका मुझे बहुत अच्छा था।उनका व्यवहार सबों के साथ बहुत अच्छा था।बोलने से पहले किसको क्या बोलना है तभी बोलते थे।इसलिए सबके प्रिय थे। उनका कहना था कि समझदार लोग ज्यादा सुनते हैं और बोलते कम हैं। इसलिए नाती भी कुछ समझाता या कुछ बोलता था तो ध्यान से सुनते थे।और अमल भी करते थे जैसे तबियत के बारे में हो या खाने पहनने के बारे में।बड़ों, छोटों सबका बाद गौर से सुनते थे।एक आदर्श शिक्षक थे उनकी इतना अच्छा पढ़ाते थे। ये मैट्रिक के विधयार्थी को इतना अच्छा प्रश्नों का चुनाव करते थे, क्योंकि विधयार्थी परीक्षा में प्रथम

क्लास से उत्तीर्ण हो जाता था जो उनके हाथ से विद्यार्थी मैट्रिक, इंटर तथा कोई नौकरी का फार्म भरवाता था।

श्रीमती रशिम रानी, शिक्षिका, मध्य विद्यालय, बाघी, बेगुसराय (छोटी दीदी)

पापा ने यह सुनिश्चित किया कि मैं और मेरी बहन दोनों को अन्य बच्चों की तरह ही शिक्षा मिले। मेरे माता-पिता दोनों हमारे शिक्षक थे। मैंने गाँव के एक स्कूल में पढ़ाई की | पापा का जीवन और दिनचर्या मेरे लिए हमेशा प्रेरणादायक था| पापा चाहते थे कि हम डॉक्टर बनें, यही मेरा भी लगातार मदद करते रहे

प्रशिक्षण पूरा करने के बाद, मुझे बिहार में नियमों के अनुसार सरकारी स्कूल में एक शिक्षण पद के लिए प्रतीक्षा सूची में रखा गया था। जब पापा को पता चला कि मेरी ज्वाइनिंग में कुछ साल की देरी हो सकती है, तो उन्होंने प्रतियोगी परीक्षाओं की तैयारी के लिए कहा,यह मेरे लिए चुनौतीपूर्ण था क्योंकि मेरे ऊपर दो छोटे बच्चों की महत्वपूर्ण ज़िम्मेदारियाँ थीं।

अंत में, मुझे बेगुसराय के एक सरकारी मिडिल स्कूल में शिक्षक के रूप में एक शिक्षक का पद मिल गया। जहां मैं अब अपने परिवार का भरण-पोषण करने मे अपने पति की सहभागनी बनी | मैंने अपने 2 बच्चों को पढ़ाया, उनमें से एक को सार्वजनिक क्षेत्र की कंपनी (ओएनजीसी की सहायक कंपनी) में अच्छी नौकरी मिल गई और दूसरा मेडिकल प्रवेश परीक्षा की तैयारी कर रहा है। पापा की वजह से ही आज हम अच्छी जिंदगी जी रहे हैं। “जीवन की अब अनियंत्रित ऊर्जा को।नियंत्रित कर जीवन को सही दिशा सवस्थ जीवन, लंबी उम्र एवं सफलताओं का अंबार लगाने की दिशा में।अग्रसर रहने के लिए वे प्रेरित करते थे।और वे घर, परिवार से लेकर समाज, कस्बे के बच्चे, बच्ची, युवति, युवकों को शिक्षा के लिए हमेशा चलते फिरते प्रोत्साहित करते रहते थे और जीवन के अंतिम क्षण तक वे शिक्षा का दान देते रहे।वह

एक योग प्रधानाध्यापक के साथ बड़े ही कुशल एवं बेहतरीन अभिभावक भी थे।जिनके सफल एवं कुशल नेतृत्व के कारण ही हमेशा कर्मानुसार हमलोग इतने आगे बढ़ते रहें।वे प्राथमिक विद्यालय तुनियाही से चौथी एवं पांचवी कक्षा की पढ़ाई की, उसके बाद MPHS इंटरमीडिएट इंटर स्तरीय मल्टीपर्पस हायर सेकेंडरी विद्यालय मधेपुरा से पूर्ण पढ़ाई करने के बाद आगे की पढ़ाई कॉलेज बेगूसराय एवं अन्य स्थानों से पूरी किया। बेगूसराय में महा विद्यालय में पढ़ाई करने के दौरान ही उनकी शादी बेगूसराय में संपन्न।सोनपुर में शिक्षा विभाग के संगठन के अधिकारी के रूप में।वे कुशल नेतृत्व प्रदान किए।"

श्री अजीत कुमार सिन्हा (सेवानिवृत्त कार्यालय अधीक्षक, उत्तरी रेल प्रधान कार्यालय, दिल्ली

आज हम एक ऐसे शख्सियत के बारे में बात करने जा रहे हैं जो अपने जीवनकाल में सीमित प्रकृति, परिवारिक और सामाजिक संसाधन का उपयोग कर अपने शैक्षणिक योग्यता, अनुभव और मेहनत द्वारा करीब 60 वर्ष अपने परिवार और समाज की अविस्मरणीय सेवा प्रदान किए। वे हमारे श्रद्धेय, आदरणीय, सम्माननीय "केशव बाबू" है।जिन्हे हम अपने परिवार में बड़का मेहमान के नाम से संबोधित करते हैं।उन्हें बाल काल से पढ़ने पढ़ाने का शौक था। वे उच्च शिक्षा गणेश दत्त महाविद्यालय,बेगूसराय करने के पश्चात मनोकूल जीवन संगिनी हमारी बड़ी दीदी (श्रीमती रुक्मिणी कुमारी) के साथ शिक्षा क्षेत्र में क़दम रखे। वे बहुत ही अल्प आयु में अपने प्रतिभा, योग्यता से जंग बहादुर सिंह कन्या माध्यमिक विद्यालय के प्रधानाध्यापक बने।जो अभी राजकीय माध्यमिक कन्या विद्यालय के नाम से सुचारू रूप से चल रही है। यह. विद्यालय उस समय के काल खंड हरिहर क्षेत्र में प्रथम कन्या मध्य विद्यालय रहा होगा।यह विद्यालय महिला सशक्तिकरण में एक अभूतपूर्व भूमिका निभा रहा है। उनसें हमारा पारिवारिक संबंध रहने के कारण उन्हें मुझे बहुत नजदीकी से जाननें, समझने तथा

सिखने का ज्ञान प्राप्त हुआ | परिवार के वरिष्ठ सदस्य के नाते मेरे ही नहीं परिवार के सभी सदस्यों के संरक्षक, अभिभावक, मार्गदर्शक थे | उनके तथा बड़ी दीदी के मार्गदर्शन में हम सभी नवो भाई और बहनों (६बहने+३भाईयों) का पढ़ाई लिखाई हुआ । तथा इनके दिशानिर्देश से तीन बहनें मुन्ना दीदी, गुड़ी दीदी और आशा दीदी सरकारी शिक्षिका सेवा में प्रतिनिधित्व की। बाबू जी घर के सभी कार्य में उनका राय मशवरा आवश्यक लिया करते थे। वे बहुमुखी व्यक्तित्व के धनी पुरुष थे|

उनकी पहचान केवल शिक्षा के क्षेत्र में ही नहीं था।बल्कि वे समाजिक, वैवाहिक, सामाजिक सुधार कार्यक्रम में बढ़ चढ़कर भाग लेते थे।वे अनगिनत अपने परिवार एवं समाज के सभी वर्ग के शादी करने योग्य लड़का लड़की ठीक करने में योगदान किए | उन्हें कभी गुस्सा करते नहीं देखा या यो कहे की उनके मैथिली भाषा में गुस्सा पर भी मुसकुराहट की अनुभूति होता था " ऐनही काम करह छि..." | मैथली क्षेत्र के वासी रहने के कारण उनकी भाषा व्यवहार बहुत ही मधुर था |उनका रहन- सहन बहुत साधारण था परन्तु सफाई एवं स्वच्छता के बहुत प्रेमी थे। उनका नित्य दिन का कार्य सुबह 5:00 बजे से रात्रि 10:00 बजे तक बिलकुल समयबद्ध अनुसार योग, साधना, पूजा, स्नान, भोजन तथा शिक्षण आदि कार्य संपन्न करते थे। वे पान खाने के बहुत ही प्रेमी थे उन्हें पान खिलाकर आप उन्हें अपनी ओर सम्मोहित कर सकते थे। परमात्मा की दया से उनको दो सुपुत्री(डेजी और कमकम) एक सुपुत्र (सिट्टू)है। दोनों लड़कियां स्नातकोत्तर शिक्षा ग्रहण कर सरकारी स्कूल में शिक्षिका है और पुत्र चण्डीगढ़ यूनिवर्सिटी से एम फार्मा तथा अस्ट्रेलिया से डऔक्टेरट कर वेलजियम में वरिष्ठ वैज्ञानिक पद पर सुशोभित हैं,इस तरह उन्होंने जीवन की यात्रा एक दूरस्थ अविकसित ग्राम वुधामा से विकसित देश अस्ट्रेलिया और वेलजियम तक की।वे बहुत हर्षित और गौरांवित अनुभूति किए जब उनके पुत्र का पत्रकार द्वारा साक्षात्कार "गुदरी का लाल" हिन्दी दैनिक समाचार पत्र में प्रकाशित हुआ। वे पूर्ण रूप से संतुष्ट जीवन यापन करते हुए सुबह ४ मार्च २०२३ पूजा करने के पश्चात चलते फिरते 80 बर्ष के आयु में ब्रह्मलीन हो गए।

उनका अभाव हमारे जीवन तथा परिवार के अप्राप्य क्षति है, उनकी याद अविस्मरणीय है।

सादर कोटी कोटी नमन्

श्री राकेश राज सिंह (गुल्लू भैया)

हमारे प्रिय सर "केशव मास्टर साहब"

माँ बाप हमें जन्म देते हैं तो शिक्षक हमारे जीवन में सफल बनाते।शिक्षक हमारे जीवन में महत्वपूर्ण भूमिका निभाते हैं।वे हमें पढ़ाई के साथ साथ जीवन जीने की कला भी सिखाते हैं।शिक्षक हमें पढ़ाते हैं।ज्ञान देते हैं। हमें पढ़ाकर एक अच्छा नागरिक बनने मे सहयोग करते हैं, शिक्षक ही हमारा भविष्य बनाते हैं, शिक्षकों को ईश्वर का दर्जा दिया जाता है।

वैसे तो मेरे जीवन में कई अध्यापक हैं और सभी मुझे बहुत पसंद है, लेकिन उन सब में मेरे सबसे प्रिय शिक्षक थे हमारे गांव के सर " केशव मास्टर साहब" वे एक आदर्श शिक्षक थे।

केशव सर स्वभाव से सरल, शांत और विनर्म थे। उनका व्यक्तित्व बहुत प्रभावित था परंतु वे समय के बड़े पाबंद थे ।उनका बाहरी व्यतित्वा जितना सुंदर और आकर्षक था, उतना ही उनका स्वभाव अच्छा और मिलनसार था।उनका मानना था कि जीवन के प्रति हमें सकारात्मक सोच रखनी चाहिए।हमारे मार्ग में कोई भी चुनौती आए उनका डटकर मुकाबला करना चाहिए।उनके जीवन में अनुशासन का बड़ा महत्त्व था। वह हमें सदा अच्छी राह पर चलने का संदेह देते थे। हमारी गलती होने पर वे हमें प्रेम से समझाते थे।वे हमें समय समय पर आगे बढ़ने के लिए मार्गदर्शन करते थे। सर जी जब ज्यादा गुस्सा होते थे तो उनका एक शब्द "भुस्गोल, काम धंधा कुछ नहीं फुटानी लंबा चौरा काम चोर", बोलते थे, जो शब्द मुझे आज भी याद रहता है।लेकिन उनके गुस्से पर भी हमें मुस्कुराहट और हँसी आ जाती थी।

केशव सर हमारे क्षेत्र पूरे सोनपुर के बहुत ही प्रसिद्ध शिक्षक थे। हमारे गांव के साथ साथ पूरे सोनपुर के हर घर के चहेते

शिक्षक थे इसी कारण हर माता पिता की हार्दिक इच्छा होता था की केशव सर से ही मेरे बच्चे को पढ़ाएं, जिनमें उनके उज्ज्वल भविष्य बनाने में मददगार साबित हो

हमारे घर के सारे बच्चे पिछले 40 वर्षों से लेकर अभी तक शिक्षा केशव सर से लिया| जिसमे मेरी बड़ी बहन, दीदी, बड़ा भाई और मेरी छोटी बहन के साथ साथ मुझे सर जी से पढ़ने का सौभाग्य प्राप्त हुआ। आज हमारे पास जो भी शिक्षा के रूप में ज्ञान है, उसका शुरुआत का श्रेय केशव सर को ही जाता है। उन्हें कई विषयों का अच्छा ज्ञान था। उसमें अंग्रेजी भाषा का बहुत अच्छा ज्ञान था। उनके पढ़ाने का तरीका बहुत सरल था। वे हम लोगों को समय समय पर आगे बढ़ने के लिए मार्गदर्शक का भी काम करते थे। वे हमें पढ़ाई के साथ साथ जीवन जीने की कला भी सिखाते थे

एक साल की बात है कि हमारे गांव में प्रत्येक साल दुर्गापूजा का आयोजन किया जाता था। जिस पूजा के लिए पूरे ग्रामवासी द्वारा एक कमिटी (समिति) का गठन किया जाता है जिसमें एक बार 2017 में केशव सर के नेतृत्व में समिति का गठन हुआ। उस समिति में कोषाध्यक्ष के रूप में सरजी का चुनाव हुआ। उस समिति में एक सदस्य के रूप में मुझे भी काम करने का मौका मिला था। पूजा की तैयारी शुरू हुई और माँ दुर्गा के आशीर्वाद से सब कुछ सही सही होते हुए पूजा सम्पन्न हुआ। प्रत्येक साल की तरह इस बार भी पूजा संपन्न होने के बाद जब खर्चे का हिसाब हुआ तो उस सबसे ज्यादा रुपया (1,84, 365) बचा जो अभी तक के इतिहास में उतना रुपया कोई भी समिति ने बचाकर नहीं दिया था जो केशव सर के कोषाध्यक्ष के समय में बचा| मैं बहुत भाग्यशाली हूँ कि मुझे केशव सर के रूप में शिक्षक मिले और उनका अनुभव आदर, सम्मान करता हूँ। मैं उन्हें भगवान की तरह रखता हूँ।आज मैं जो भी हूँ मेरे शिक्षक की वजह से।

सीमांत सिंह गौतम (बंटू)

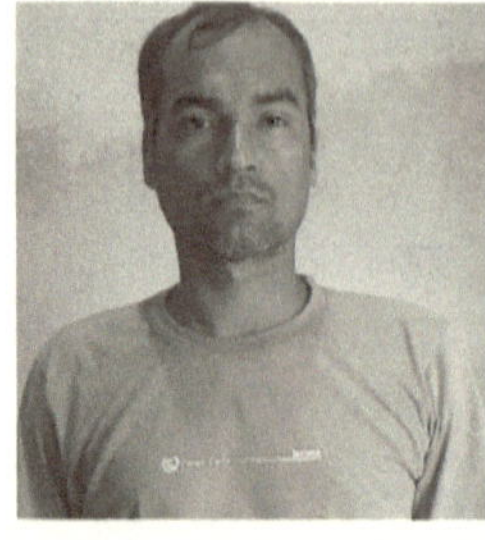

है कि जो मानव इस पृथिव में जन्म दिया है, उसका जाना निश्चित है | उनका निधन मेरी व्यक्तिगत क्षति है। बचपन से लेकर जवानी तक मैंने उनका अनुसरण किया।भविष्य में भी करता रहूंगा। उनका पूरा जीवन एक खुली किताब की तरह था जिसे कोई भी सरलता पूर्वक पढ़ सकता था। अध्यापन पेशा कौन उन्होने इतनी उचाई प्रदान की कि कोई भी उन्हें नज़र नज़र अंदाज़ नहीं कर सकता। हमेशा से मैंने उनके अंदर जोश जज्बे को देखता था जो यह दर्शाता था कि व्यक्ति एक निरंतर एवं अनवरत कार्यशील प्राणी है।

सेवानिवृत्त होने के बाद भी वह लगातार अध्ययन कार्यों मे पूरी तरह से लग्न थे। हमारे पहाड़ीचक बालिका विद्यालय के जो भी शिक्षकगण को किसी भी समस्या में होते थे, वे सदैव उन्हें ही स्मरण करते थे। उनका व्यक्तित्व अनुभव इतना व्यापक था कि हर कोई उनके सलाह मसौरा के लिए संपर्क करता था। उनकी सबसे बड़ी खासियत थी कि वे कभी भी चिंता नहीं रखते होते थे, ना ही कभी तनाव में रहने रहते थे। शिक्षण पेशा को उन्होंने पूरी शिद्धत पूर्वक किया और साबित करता है की इंसान का कर्म ही उसे महान बनाता है। मैंने उनके साथ काफी सालों तक अध्यापन भी किया और उनसे प्रेरित भी होता रहा।वर्ग के सभी छात्र छात्राएं भी बड़ी सहजता पूर्वक अपनी बातों को उन से समझ।रखती थी। हर किसी वर्ग के साथ उनका दोस्ताना व्यवहार एक समान था। हर वर्ग में उनकी एक समान प्रतिष्ठा थी जो यह बताता है कि वह सभी वर्गों में काफी लोकप्रिय थे, उनसे ही प्रभावित होकर मैंने अध्यापनशुरू किया। अक्सर मैं उनसे सलाह लिया करता था, जिससे वे काफी प्रसन्न होते थे।

उनका निधन की भरपाई बहुत ही मुश्किल है। उनके आदर्श सदैव मेरे साथ रहेंगी और मैं उनसे प्रेरणा लेता रहूंगा। उन्हीं के कारण मैं भी सहजता एवं सरलता से हर समस्याओं को सुलझाता

हूँ। उन्होंने मुझे धैर्यवान बना दिया कि मुझे कभीभी कोई समस्या का अहसास ही नहीं होता।वे अक्सर कहते थे कि कोई भी काम में इतना रम जाओ कि वह काम तुम्हारा शौक बन जाए।जिससे करते रहे। तुम्हें आनंद की अनुभूति हो। आज भी मैं उनकी बातों को अपने पूरे जीवन में आत्मसात किया हुआ है, जिससे मुझे कभी कोई तकलीफ नहीं होती औरक्या लिखूं उनके व्यक्तित्व के बारे में शायद मुझे नहीं पता, जितना लिखूंगा उतना कम है। उनका विराट सदा मुझे प्रेरित करता रहेगा।

सत्यप्रकाश सिंह

केशव सर, एक ऐसे व्यक्ति जिनके बारे में जितना कहा जाए कम है।जिन की असमय मृत्यु से मैं काफी हताहत हूँ।जिन्होंने कभी भी अपने आप को रिटायर्ड नहीं समझा। जिन्होंने अपने पूरे जीवन काल को शिक्षा कार्य के लिए और शिक्षण कार्य के प्रति समर्पित कर दिया। शिक्षा से जुड़े कोई भी कार्य हो उन्होंने कभी भी किसी को ना नहीं कहें।

मैं स्वयं भी उनके साथ शिक्षण कार्य में 14-15 वर्षों तक जुड़ा रहा। मैंने कभी भी उनको थकते हुए नहीं देखा। मेरा उनके साथ लगाव काफी गहरा था। वे हमेशा मेरे लिए प्रेरणा के स्रोत बने रहे; जिन्होंने अपने अनुभव से मेरा शिक्षण कौशल को निखारा।

एक बार हुए हम युवाओं के साथ पूजा कमिटी दुर्गा पूजा से भी जुड़े और बहुत ही जोशीला ढंग से कार्य किए और उस साल का पूजा और चंदा हमारे चरम स्तर पर था।ऐसे महान व्यक्ति को मेरा बार बार परिणाम, सत्यप्रकाश सिंह।

मुझे जब उनके गुज़रने की खबर मिली तो मैं बहुत स्तब्ध रह गई और विश्वास ही नहीं हो रहा था | कैसे क्या हुआ?इसकी जानकारी ली । जब जब उनकी याद आती है तो आँखे नम हो जाती है और उनके साथ बिताया हुआ समय याद आ जाती है। उनका जो सहयोग हम लोग को मिला उसको कभी भूल नहीं सकते

हैं। छात्राओं, शिक्षक और शिक्षिकाओं सभी को रिटायर होने के 20 सालों तक सहयोग करते रहे। उनकी खूबियाँ लोगों को हमेशा याद दिलाती रहेगी । ऐसे लोग कम होते हैं। उनकी याद हमारे दिल में हमेशा रहेगा। यही मेरी श्रद्धांजलि हैं

About the Author

Dr. Gaurav Kumar currently holds the position of Associate Director in the Medical Affairs division of a reputable pharmaceutical company based in Belgium, where he has resided for the past 15 years.

Born and raised in Sonpur (Saran), Bihar, Dr. Kumar completed his primary and middle school education in the village. A dedicated student with aspirations of becoming a doctor, he journeyed to Delhi to complete his 10th and 12th grades at a government school in East Delhi from 1989-1993. Despite facing challenges, his determination led him to excel. Dr. Kumar completed his bachelor's degree in pharmacy, ranking first in the university over the four-year program at North Maharashtra University (Jalgaon).

Qualifying with an impressive 97.3 percentile in the GATE exam, he earned a scholarship for his master's degree at Panjab University, Chandigarh, specializing in Pharmacology. Following his education in India, Dr. Kumar was honored with the prestigious Melbourne International Research Fellowship award, which facilitated his pursuit of a Ph.D. in Neuropharmacology at the

University of Melbourne, Australia. Before embarking on his Ph.D., he also served as a lecturer in the Department of Pharmacy at a respected government-funded institution in Indore for two years.

Throughout his academic journey, Dr. Kumar achieved excellence, being the university topper in B. Pharmacy and obtaining a remarkable 97 percentile in the national-level Graduate Aptitude Test in Engineering (GATE). He has received numerous awards and published peer-reviewed articles on his research in epilepsy and cognitive disorders in esteemed international journals.

लेखक के बारे में

डॉ. गौरव कुमार वर्तमान में बेल्जियम स्थित एक प्रतिष्ठित फार्मास्युटिकल कंपनी के मेडिकल अफेयर्स डिवीजन में एसोसिएट डायरेक्टर के पद पर हैं, जहां वे पिछले 15 वर्षों से रह रहे हैं।

बिहार के सोनपुर (सारण) में जन्मे और पले-बढ़े डॉ. कुमार ने अपनी प्राथमिक और मध्य विद्यालय की शिक्षा गाँव में पूरी की। डॉक्टर बनने की आकांक्षा रखने वाले एक समर्पित छात्र, उन्होंने 1989-1993 तक पूर्वी दिल्ली के एक सरकारी स्कूल में अपनी 10वीं और 12वीं कक्षा पूरी करने के लिए दिल्ली की यात्रा की। चुनौतियों का सामना करने के बावजूद, उनके दृढ़ संकल्प ने उन्हें उत्कृष्टता हासिल करने के लिए प्रेरित किया। डॉ. कुमार ने उत्तर महाराष्ट्र विश्वविद्यालय (जलगांव) में चार साल के कार्यक्रम में विश्वविद्यालय में प्रथम स्थान प्राप्त करते हुए फार्मेसी में स्नातक की डिग्री पूरी की।

GATE परीक्षा में प्रभावशाली 97.3 प्रतिशत अंक के साथ उत्तीर्ण होकर, उन्होंने पंजाब विश्वविद्यालय, चंडीगढ़ में फार्माकोलॉजी में विशेषज्ञता के साथ अपनी मास्टर डिग्री के लिए छात्रवृत्ति अर्जित की। भारत में अपनी शिक्षा के बाद, डॉ. कुमार को प्रतिष्ठित मेलबर्न इंटरनेशनल रिसर्च फ़ेलोशिप पुरस्कार से सम्मानित किया गया, जिससे उन्हें पीएचडी करने में आसानी हुई। अपनी पीएचडी शुरू करने से पहले, उन्होंने दो साल तक इंदौर में

एक प्रतिष्ठित सरकारी वित्त पोषित संस्थान में फार्मेसी विभाग में व्याख्याता के रूप में भी काम किया।

अपनी शैक्षणिक यात्रा के दौरान, डॉ. कुमार ने उत्कृष्टता हासिल की, बी. फार्मेसी में विश्वविद्यालय के टॉपर रहे और राष्ट्रीय स्तर के ग्रेजुएट एप्टीट्यूड टेस्ट इन इंजीनियरिंग (गेट) में उल्लेखनीय 97 प्रतिशत अंक प्राप्त किए। उन्हें कई पुरस्कार प्राप्त हुए हैं और प्रतिष्ठित अंतरराष्ट्रीय पत्रिकाओं में मिर्गी और संज्ञानात्मक विकारों पर उनके शोध पर सहकर्मी-समीक्षित लेख प्रकाशित हुए हैं।

Contact details of author:

Email address: gkumar_discovery@yahoo.com

Linkedin: https://www.linkedin.com/in/gaurav-kumar-557b2318b?utm_source=share&utm_campaign=share_via&utm_content=profile&utm_medium=ios_app

fb: https://www.facebook.com/gauravkumarscientist

www.ingramcontent.com/pod-product-compliance
Lightning Source LLC
LaVergne TN
LVHW091104150826
845673LV00002B/716
9798892773072